The Holy and the
Hereafter
or is it Hooey?

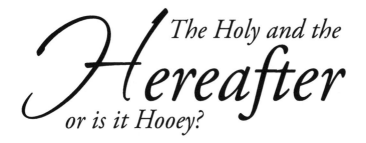

The Holy and the
Hereafter
or is it Hooey?

J L Miller

iUniverse LLC
Bloomington

The Holy and the Hereafter or is it Hooey?

iUniverse books may be ordered through booksellers or by contacting:

iUniverse LLC
1663 Liberty Drive
Bloomington, IN 47403
www.iuniverse.com
1-800-Authors (1-800-288-4677)

Because of the dynamic nature of the Internet, any web addresses or links contained in this book may have changed since publication and may no longer be valid. The views expressed in this work are solely those of the author and do not necessarily reflect the views of the publisher, and the publisher hereby disclaims any responsibility for them.

Any people depicted in stock imagery provided by Thinkstock are models, and such images are being used for illustrative purposes only.
Certain stock imagery © Thinkstock.

ISBN: 978-1-4917-0755-5 (sc)
ISBN: 978-1-4917-0756-2 (e)

Library of Congress Control Number: 2013916849

Printed in the United States of America

iUniverse rev. date: 10/29/2013

Table of Contents

In loving memory of my grandson

Sam

1 CONFLICTS WITH TRUTH

The year was 1951. The place was a Southern town. The drive-in movie featuring *The Thing From Another World* had just ended. My friend Garland and I quickly mounted our bicycles and headed for the exit. Vivid thoughts of this classic science fiction flick occupied our fourteen-year-old brains.

As the passed cars disappeared from view, the night itself seemed to grow blacker and blacker. The roadside trees seemed to be taking the shape of the alien monster, THE THING. Our response was to paddle faster and faster. Not a word was said: we needed every bit of energy that could be mustered to offset our increasing heart and respiratory rates.

The year was 2006 as I drove past the spot where the old drive-in movie once stood. Thoughts arose of that night some fifty-five years ago when my friend and I – fueled by the terror of a movie – covered the two miles to town in record time. In 1951 UFOs began to appear that were interpreted as alien spacecraft and movies about them were becoming a reality. The reality of the next fifty five years would provide no evidence of an actual craft or creature from other than earth origin.

The sadder reality is that Garland died several years ago. In my view his lifespan was considerably shortened due to many years of heavy smoking and little attention to healthy habits. Notwithstanding that, the male members of his family appeared to have a genetic tendency toward early death.

Over time I've learned that reality at any moment is only partial. As time moves forward, new facts and experiences adjust the reality of the past. What about the future? Over the next fifty five years reality says that me and everyone who attended the movie in 1951 would be long dead.

What is the reality of death? Generally, to be dead means to be without life. What about the reality of life after human death? For those who remain alive, reality goes on as before, except that the dead no longer play an active role in one's life. At times, the living do adjust their actions to compensate for the loss of the departed. Some mourn, some visit graves; some spiral into depression or even attempt to communicate with the deceased, usually with the help of a medium. Others move on with their lives, recognizing that the dead who were a substantial part of their past can play no part in their future except in memory. Thus, they may socialize more, remarry, travel, show an interest in new ideas or turn their attention to subjects that caught their fancy long ago. With the loss of a child or special friend, only time can soften the lingering pain.

For those who have experienced death, do they ever experience anything else? Is there a soul or spirit of a person that does experience something after the physical death of the body? In reality, no living being – regardless of the religious belief, or no religious belief – can answer that question. Any claims about the hereafter are, in reality, only human speculation.

Some have thought the proof was found in many reports of near-death experiences (NDEs). In a near death experience one enters a tunnel leading to beautiful light, peace and joy. But, reality says this is proof only of how some living brains, or minds – which may not be the same thing – respond to an experience of near death. Of course, some that have experienced near death have had very negative experiences.

There are also cases of people having an NDE while connected to a brain wave machine. Despite the machine's registering no brain wave activity, these patients experienced very vivid images. These patients lived to describe the experience. Some have thought this was further proof of consciousness surviving death. But no one can say if what was recalled happened before the brain was void of activity or after the brain became active again, before the patients became fully conscious. In any case, since the people lived to tell the story, there is nothing but a possibility that NDEs tell us anything about actual death experience. Actual death does not allow a return to physical life – at least, not in our life as we know it. Many Christians, who consist of roughly one third of the world's population, may take issue by proclaiming that Jesus physically died and returned to physical life. They also say that Jesus raised others from death. Their proof is that the Bible tells them so. They accept the Bible as God's word and by what authority can I question God's word?

The Bible claims other instances of the dead returning to physical life by the intervention of holy men. Elijah, Elisha, Peter and Paul are each credited with raising the dead. Matthew 27:52-53 says after Jesus' resurrection many saints came out of their graves and went into the holy city of Jerusalem and that many people are said to have seen this amazing event.

The raising of many people at the same time echoes a similar story from the Old Testament. Ezekiel 37 tells us that God had Ezekiel raise a whole valley of dry bones back to a vast multitude of living beings. Ezekiel says he was set down in the valley by the Lord laying his hand upon him and bringing him out by the spirit of the Lord. This type of enigmatic language is used throughout the book of Ezekiel. Generally, this story is interpreted as a vision, its meaning found in the context of the rest of the chapter that addresses the issue of God uniting the house of Israel and their land.

Are either of these stories of mass returns from death true? If not, then both Old and New Testaments have at minimum a fabricated story – an untruth. The obscure text of Ezekiel may justify relegating it to a vision, not an actual event. Matthew's saints coming back to life can only be seen, and is generally interpreted, as factual, especially since only one verse separates this saying from Matthew 27:50, which tells of Jesus taking His last breath.

In the New Testament the three synoptic gospels contain many parallel passages. So why is Matthew the only one to mention this spectacular story? Likewise, why is it not found in the gospel of John? John's is the only gospel to say anything about Jesus' raising of Lazarus – arguably the second most popular story of the dead returning to life. Note that Matthew 27:52 has the graves opened and saints raised immediately after Jesus' death, which occurred on a Friday afternoon. Yet verse 53 does not have them leaving the cemetery and going into the city until after Jesus' resurrection, which happened early on Sunday. So, did the raised saints stay just in the cemetery for almost two days?

Reality and logic of present times tell us neither of these mass raising events ever actually happened. They were embellishments or distorted facts related to stories the writers were so passionate about. The two days lag in the raised saints leaving their graves demonstrates the passion that Jesus must be the first one to be fully resurrected. This again begs the question, "By what authority can I say that?" The answer is by my own authority to reason and think with intellectual honesty. I don't know how most Bible defenders reason and think, but I can say many teach and write with intellectual dishonesty. They begin from a prejudice that their religious beliefs are absolute truth and all facts or evidence is made to conform with their beliefs. Take, for example, the biblical teaching that Jesus rose on the third day which is usually attributed to the Hebrew day's beginning at sundown. So, Friday is the first day, sundown Friday to sundown Saturday is the second day and Sunday, the third day. However, Matthew 12:40 presents a problem for this explanation as it has Jesus predicting He will specifically be three days and three nights in the heart of the earth, just as Jonah spent three days and three nights in the belly of the whale. To overcome the three nights some see this as not literal, but as an idiom, that is, the ordinary meaning of a phrase that cannot be understood from its words. Of course, an idiom could be declared as an explanation for any saying that is in obvious conflict with what one prefers to believe.

Consider the first two chapters of Genesis. In chapter one God plainly creates the animals before Adam and Eve. In chapter two, man is clearly created before the animals; Eve is created after the animals. At least one version is untrue.

How do Bible defenders deal with such untruth? Dr. Henry H. Halley, author of *Halley's Bible Handbook*, which continues in publication after some 80 years and has sold millions of copies, sees chapter two as supplemental, not contradictory. He says, "Added details are not contradictions." Although the contradiction is unquestionably there, Dr. Halley refused to see it. This is a good example of what I call "intellectual dishonesty."

Certainly, most of the explanations from Bible experts are honest and useful, but many deal with contradictions, untruth, and difficult sayings either with a lot of verbiage and references that never specifically answer the question or by simply ignoring them. Take the four authors of *Hard Sayings of the Bible*. They devote nine pages of commentary to the first two chapters of Genesis. An entire page is spent on the subject of Adam's rib. What do they say about this hardest saying of two contradicting one? Nothing! Were they intellectually dishonest or were they honest enough to recognize that no amount of commentary would make both versions true?

Most Bible-based Christian attacks on Darwin and evolution theory use chapter one of Genesis to support their claim. From chapter two they pick and choose details, but usually ignore the part about man existing before the animals. Well-documented science reveals some animal types existed hundreds of millions of years before the first humans.

Intellectual dishonesty is essentially a standard technique of Bible defenders who often only quote Bible verses that support their position while ignoring verses that challenge it.

Curiously, the first chapter of the New Testament in the gospel of Matthew gives a genealogy of Jesus that ends with

Joseph and Mary, Jesus' Mother. If this is true, it would render the major disclosure in verse 20 of the same chapter untrue: that of Jesus being conceived by the Holy Spirit, which would preclude Joseph having any part in Jesus' genealogy.

In chapter three of Luke it has Jesus as the thought-to-be son of Joseph, then goes on to give a genealogy of Joseph that is somewhat different than Matthew's. The two gospels even disagree on Joseph's father: Matthew says Jacob and Luke says Heli. So, plainly, the Bible has some untruth in the beginning chapters of the Old and New Testaments. How does Halley's *Handbook* deal with the genealogy problem? It has the commonly accepted view that Matthew gives Joseph's line with Jesus being the legal heir to the promises God gave Abraham and David. Luke is said to give Mary's bloodline of descent. Since Luke never mentions Mary in his genealogy, Halley explains that this is in accord with Jewish usage, Mary's genealogy being in her husband's name. So when Luke says Joseph was the son of Heli, it really means Joseph was the son-in-law of Heli.

Honesty says if Joseph was the legal or adopted father of Jesus and not his biological father, then the first sentence of the New Testament is untrue in claiming to be an account of Jesus' genealogy. On the other hand, if it is truth that Joseph is Jesus' biological father, then Matthew's and Luke's claim of the Holy Spirit being the Fatherly source of Jesus is untrue. Halley's position that Luke is really giving Mary's line justified as Jewish usage is pure speculation. Other than these contradicting lineages, there is no Biblical support as to who was the father of either Joseph or Mary. Catholic tradition, whose authority is considered by Catholicism as equal to that of the Bible, says Mary's parents were Joachim and Ann. If true, this would prove that Luke is not giving Mary's genealogy. By Halley's reasoning, Matthew violated Jewish usage by mentioning Mary as well as other women in his genealogy; In fact, in comparing older Bibles to modern versions, there appears to be reason to disregard Luke's genealogy altogether. Halley's appeal to Jewish usage in putting the woman in the name of her husband is violated in Luke's own genealogy. In the *King James Bible* the name Joanna appears three times in the entire text, all in Luke. Verses 8:3 and 24:10 plainly refer to a woman. In 3:27 Luke's genealogy includes Joanna, who is said to be the son of Rhesa.

The New King James Bible translators knew this was a problem and try and sound more masculine by adding an "s." Thus, Joanna becomes Joannas. Modern Bibles read Joanan. This change in spelling applies only to Luke 3:27. All Bibles I consulted stay within the original spelling in the other two verses.

Perhaps the authors of Matthew and Luke should have taken Paul's advice not to occupy themselves with myths and endless genealogies that promote speculations (1 Timothy 1:3-4). In Titus 3:9 Paul says to avoid genealogies – among other things – for they are unprofitable and worthless. Does *Hard Sayings of the Bible* help with this problem? In its 800 or so pages I found nothing addressing this particular issue of genealogy.

It is not my purpose to insult anyone's Biblical beliefs, only to show that when searching for truth, intellectual dishonesty or ignoring difficult sayings will only promote error or untruth. Honesty shows that many verses of the Bible are in serious conflict with other verses that are thought to be the word of God. The main point being: Bible verses are not always true. This applies even after appeals to analogy, metaphor, or other figures of speech have been exhausted. Thus, I say the Bible is not necessarily reliable to answer the question of the reality of life after actual death.

If the Bible cannot give the answer to post-death experience, who or what can? But for now, I will explore the Bible further, mainly the Bible's relationship with truth – at least, to truth as generally taught.

I have already discussed the Bible defeating some of its own disclosures in the beginning of both Testaments. Much

Bible truth is taught from the perspective that authorities are needed to find the deeper meaning of the literal text that appears to present problems. My experience indicates that many of these experts resort to intellectual dishonesty or ignore difficult verses. I gave examples of each. Most Bible study books often use both techniques. Take, for example, the Zondervan *King James Version Study Bible* (2002). The jacket cover says "over 20,000 study notes." Hosea 13:4 reads, "Yet I am the Lord thy God from the land of Egypt, and thou shalt know no god but me: for there is no saviour beside me."

My first thought about this verse is "Does it cast doubt on Jesus as the savior over 700 years in the future?" I expected the study note to defend the saying with a trinity concept, such as God and Jesus are one and the same. Instead, the study note avoids anything about the concept of "No saviour beside me" and focuses on "I am the Lord thy God from the land of Egypt," then gives three other verses relating to God from Egypt to contrast with King Jeroboam's doings in 1 Kings 12:28 in which the King made two calves of gold and said: "Behold thy gods, O Israel, which brought thee up out of the land of Egypt." I don't understand the value of comparing what God is supposed to have said with this silly statement of Jeroboam. The study note ends with three more references to verses in Hosea about know no god. The study note was apparently meant to explain about God being from Egypt. Even with all its references to other verses, it clarified nothing for me. Usually it is assumed the concept of 'God from Egypt' signifies the Exodus.

Two other Bible verses – Isaiah 43:11 and 45:21 – also have God saying there is no savior besides him. 45:21 has no comment on the concept of savior in its study note. On 43:11 the study note advises to see verse 3 and its note. Isaiah 43:3 has God addressing Himself, "the Holy One of Israel, thy saviour." The footnote explains savior as "who delivers from the oppression of Egypt or Babylon and from the spiritual oppression of sin." The point being that the study Bible ignores any commentary about Israel's God being the only savior, which would eliminate the need for a future savior, yet works in the Christian theme of delivery from sin. Some Bible literalists teach that these Old Testament verses that have God declaring Himself as the only Savior are actually proof that Jesus is God. I see this as a good example of making the evidence fit a preconceived belief. Consider that Christian theologians decided Jesus was God many hundreds of years after Hosea or Isaiah did their preaching and since they have God saying He is the only Savior, then Jesus must be God in the eyes of some literalists.

Consider problems concerning Bible stories of how they are understood. One may consult his or her own intelligence or trusted authorities as to truth. If original sin theory is a fact, why did God's chosen people – the Hebrews – never know about it until Christian theologians started teaching this concept?

Why is it not plainly stated in the Old Testament? Jews were never looking for a Messiah to take away sin caused by Adam and Eve. They were expecting a Messiah to defeat their enemies and remove physical hardships.

Jews see Moses as the greatest and possibly holiest of God's people. Excepting Jesus, Christians have a fairly similar view. Moses is known as God's lawgiver, particularly for having received and transmitted the ten commandments. Most of the world accepts, "Thou shalt not kill." Modern translations prefer the term murder to kill.

What is the first thing the Bible tells us about Moses' adult life? He murders an Egyptian. Why does God nowhere in the Old Testament take Moses to task for that deed? Since this took place before his giving of the law, did God just forgive and forget?

God was surely hard on Moses at times: like, denying him entrance into the Promised Land after forty rough years of wandering in the desert wasteland. Why? Moses was apparently punished for getting water from a rock in a different manner than the way God instructed. At least one writer takes it that way! In Numbers 20:7-12, God instructs Moses to command the rock to give water. Instead, with his staff Moses struck the rock twice. He still got water. But God says to Moses and Aaron that they did not trust him, so neither Moses nor Aaron is allowed to go into the Promised Land.

Exodus 17:6 apparently has a different author telling a similar story with God instructing Moses to strike the rock for water and he does so. This time, nothing is said about a negative consequence for Moses or Aaron.

Why did God give the Israelites a Promised Land that was already occupied and had been partially developed by other people? In taking care of his chosen people, God is said to have performed many miracles. Why did not God miraculously turn some of that wasteland into a fertile land for the Israelites? This may have avoided some very troubling events of the forty-year period, such as God commanding Moses – and later, Joshua, in the Promised Land – to slaughter the enemy men, women, children and their animals. In Exodus 32 it is the slaughter of 3,000 of Moses' own people. Why? For participating in the making of a golden calf. Why was Aaron, Moses' brother – who actually made the idol and lied to Moses, claiming it came out of the fire after gold was thrown in – not punished? Instead, he was allowed to continue as the chief priest. Yet God also refused Aaron entrance into the Promised Land, apparently because he was with Moses when Moses got water from the rock contrary to God's instruction.

Elijah's holiness is so great that he is possibly the only person in the Bible who ascended in a whirlwind to heaven without dying (2 Kings 2:11). He performed great miracles, including, among others, restoring to life a dead child, calling down fire from heaven and the parting of the Jordan River.

In 1 Kings 18:40 this great holy man, Elijah, has 450 Baal priests murdered. Why is he never chastised for that horrible deed? I said Elijah was possibly the only one to ascend in a whirlwind, but Enoch might have gone to heaven in the same way. Genesis 5:24 says that Enoch walked with God, then he was no more, because God took him. In the New Testament, Hebrews 11:5 interprets that due to Enoch's faith he did not experience death because God took him. It does not say how this was done. In my book *Mr. Adoy* there is commentary on each of the ten commandments. Bible verses are given that show God ordering Moses to break the four regarding killing, stealing, lying and making an image and I will not repeat them here.

Many problems can be found with the view of a loving God and how He is portrayed in the Old Testament. Now consider a few New Testament perplexities.

Jesus' purpose in coming to earth was to tragically die in order to redeem humankind from Adam and Eve's original sin. This is the main doctrine of Christianity. Yet the four gospels – with the exception of Matthew – never say that Jesus' Blood was shed for the forgiveness of sins. While all four gospels narrate on Jesus' Blood, and Mark 14:24 and Luke 22:20 parallel Matthew 26:28, which is the only verse that specifically has Jesus say, when offering His apostles a drink from His cup of wine, that His Blood of the Covenant is being poured out for many for the forgiveness of sins. Matthew 20:28 and Mark 10:45 say that the Son of Man came to serve and to give his life as a ransom for many.

Most independent scholars agree that Mark's gospel was the earliest one written. Since Matthew contains over ninety percent of Mark's gospel, and Luke, over fifty percent, this is evidence that Matthew and Luke got much of their information from Mark or at least from the same source that Mark used. As Matthew, Mark and Luke contain a great deal of the same information in identical or similar language, it becomes obvious there was plenty of copying from another's work. The first three gospels are known as the synoptic gospels because together they are thought to give a comprehensive view and tell a common story. Some experts explain that Mark did such a good job there was no need to duplicate his effort. An equal answer might be that the authors of Matthew and Luke had little knowledge of many events in Jesus' life.

John 1:29 declares that Jesus is the Lamb of God who takes away the sin of the world. Although this passage says nothing about blood, theologians teach that it is inferred because a lamb was a sacrificial animal. Note that John has Jesus taking away the sin of the world, while Matthew and Mark have Jesus' death limited to just being for many. Also, John 6:53-56 has Jesus apparently referring to himself as the Son of Man and giving some of the most bizarre instructions in the New Testament: that is, to eat his flesh and drink his blood, and those who do so will have eternal life. These passages are the origin of the Catholic ritual of the Eucharist. Roman Catholics, Eastern Orthodox and Lutherans believe in the real presence of Jesus at their bread and wine rituals; while other denominations that include this ceremony generally see it as symbolic of the Body and Blood of Jesus.

If Jesus really did redeem humankind from sin, why would not a divinely inspired New Testament make this greatest of teachings crystal clear in all four gospels? In fact, when Jesus was asked what is the greatest commandment, Matthew 22:37 and Mark 12:30 have Jesus answering with a quote from the Old Testament (Deuteronomy 6:5): "You shall love the Lord your God with all your heart, and with all your soul, and with all your might." The New Testament says "mind" instead of "might;" and Mark's verse adds "with all your strength." Presently, and throughout history, this commandment has been the main theme of Judaism.

Matthew and Mark also give the same second greatest commandment: "You shall love your neighbor as yourself." This teaching, too, originated in Jewish scripture of the Old Testament (Leviticus 19:18.)

John 13:34 has Jesus giving a new commandment, "To love one another, as I have loved you." Jesus then says that by following this commandment, everyone will know that you are his disciple (John 13:35.)

The theme of Christianity is that Jesus died for the redemption of our sins. The teaching is that those who do not believe and accept that fact cannot enter the kingdom of heaven; thus, many Christians believe that those non-believers are destined to go to eternal hell. However, this is in conflict with Jesus' two greatest commandments, which indicate that the Jews were already on the right path in teaching love of God and love of neighbor. Shortly, in this book, I will explore the tremendous implication of John 13:34-35.

2 BIBLICAL INSPIRATION VS. REALITY

Most scholars agree that Paul was the earliest of New Testament writers, probably composing Galatians in the late 40's. Agreement continues on Paul authoring seven of the thirteen books or letters that are generally credited to him. Extremes posit that Paul wrote as few as three books on the low end to as many as fourteen books that include Hebrews. In any case, Paul probably authored more New Testament books than any other single author; Luke's two books contain the most text by a single author – unless Paul is credited with the thirteen books, plus Hebrews.

With the exception of the Resurrection, Paul appears to be unaware of the miracles described in the four gospels.

If these miracles really occurred, why would the earliest author – generally thought by historians to report the most accurate facts, there being the least time elapsed between the event and the report – fail to disclose any of them?

Surely the most important biblical event in Paul's personal experience was his conversion to Christianity, caused by the supernatural appearance of Jesus on the Damascus road. Why do none of Paul's writings relate this experience? In 1 Corinthians 15:8 he says that Jesus appeared to him, but furnishes no details. We only know of the details second-hand from Luke in his Book of Acts. Luke thought the event so important that he tells the story three times (Chapters 9, 22 and 26). Luke was a traveling companion of Paul, after Paul's conversion. Luke was not an eyewitness to the conversion. Luke wrote the Book of Acts at the earliest in the mid-60s and more probably twenty or so years later. Paul's death is thought to have occurred around 67 C.E.

It should be made clear that no one knows exactly when any of the books of the New Testament were written, or – for sure – who wrote them. Generally, the three synoptic gospels are thought to have been written somewhere between the early 50s to late 70s. The gospel of John has supporters for an early writing in the 50s to as late as the 90s or beyond. The bottom line is that all the New Testament was written over a period of at least fifteen to seventy years after Jesus' time and Jesus Himself penned not one word of it.

The majority of Christian theology is based on the teachings of Paul. This includes Jesus' atoning death for the forgiveness of humankind's sins. My thinking is that this teaching is jumbled in the gospels because they were written during a period some years after Jesus' time. By then, Paul's preaching of Jesus' death seen as atonement was being accepted by Christian theology. These later gospel writers apparently had no first-hand knowledge of the doctrine from Jesus and did not fully grasp the teaching. Even so, their writings incorporated some elements of this theology. Possibly, editors added this at a later date. The idea of Jesus taking away the world's sins may also have originated in the Old Testament. Leviticus 16 has God giving instructions for the high priest, Aaron, to take two goats. One is to be killed as a sacrifice in atonement for all Israel. The other goat is led into the wilderness to be set free while bearing all Israel's sins and iniquities on itself.

Now consider the great expectation of Christian theology, the return of Jesus.

How can one be sure of truth vs. error in the three synoptic gospels when they are so wrong about Jesus' second coming? In almost identical language, Jesus proclaims His returning would take place during the lifetime of at least some of His contemporaries (Matthew 16:28; Mark 9:1; and Luke 9:27).

Paul seems to agree with this view. 1 Corinthians 7:25-31 has Paul advising people to remain as they are: no marriage or leaving a marriage; that even if married, to act as if there is no spouse. Paul saw an impending crisis that in a short time the present form of this world would be passing away. Verses 32-35 make it clear that he wants all people to have unhindered devotion to the Lord who is coming very soon.

The *King James Study Bible* experts prefer to see the above three gospel references as a prediction of the transfiguration, which happened a week or so later and which demonstrated that Jesus will return in His Father's glory (Matthew 16:27).

However, they ignore the last half of verse 16:27, which says "and then he shall reward every man according to his works." Jesus calls the transfiguration event a vision (Matthew 17:9) and as every man DID NOT receive his reward at that time, the Bible itself defeats this view of the experts.

The apostle Peter (1 Peter 4:7), the apostle John (Revelation 22:20), Jesus' brother, James (James 5:9) and the author of Hebrews 10:25 all thought that Jesus' return was imminent. The *King James Study Bible's* footnote on James 5:9 explains that the New Testament insistence on imminence comes from the teaching that the "last days" began with the incarnation of Jesus and we have been living the last days ever since. Since the last days have exceeded 720,000 in number, that now seems to be an unacceptable explanation and definitely a misnomer to call the period. Honesty better supports that most of the New Testament writers simply believed Jesus was returning at any hour, just as many evangelicals think today.

Then, there is the difference between John and the other gospels on the core of Christianity – faith. The three synoptic gospels portray most miracles – signs – as the result of someone's faith stimulating Jesus' compassion. John has miracles as the cause to have faith. Does true faith in God really have anything to do with miracles? If so, what about a seeming miracle in the present day – the fact that we are here? Some say we evolved naturally; no God was necessary. If God was our originator, would not God be the natural cause of our being here? In fact, God would be the most natural thing there is.

Paul adds another twist to faith. In 1 Corinthians 13:13, Paul says charity is greater than faith. At least, older Bibles like the *King James* put it that way. Modern Bibles read love instead of charity. In fact, whereas the *King James* uses the word charity twenty eight times, it does not appear in any modern Bible that I checked. Modern translators prefer to say love that is considered in present times to be a synonym for charity.

Oddly, the word charity does not appear in the Old Testament, even in the *King James* or English version of the *Jewish Bible*. Yet Jews see charity as an important obligation of their faith. Some see it as mandatory, even if love is not involved.

Christianity and Judaism place great emphasis on a God of love, although some verses of the Bible appear to really jumble this message. What are we to think of a God who allows – or even orders – some of His holy men to commit mass murder? In Elijah's slaughter of the Baal priests, he does not even say this was commanded by the Lord as is the justification in some other Old Testament atrocities. Should any serious Bible student just ignore such mayhem? Or should one accept that this is God's way of punishing the wicked and no man has the right to question His methods? I say this is totally contrary to the action of love. Honesty demands that we recognize that much of the Bible was not inspired by a God of love. A God that commands or disregards mass murder by his holiest people is not a God most people would like to spend eternity with.

I think the better view is that God did not inspire the writings of the Bible to any more of a degree than He inspired the writing of this book or any other book. What we read in the Bible came from the thoughts of the biblical authors. Many penned their best understanding of God within the cultural and social fabric of their day and age. Others penned their theological prejudices of the time and did not hesitate to embellish the facts, even to miracles.

Honesty says that atrocities credited to commands of God in the Bible are still wrong and the writers who penned them should not be seen as moral teachers in our day and age. All biblical interpretations should be made based on morally acceptable principles in the present day. This does not mean that the Bible does not contain any good information for today. It means many Bible verses require that we make intelligent value judgments as to how they may best serve today's reality. For example, is there any more ridiculous instruction God is supposed to have given man than those in Ezekiel 4? God wants Ezekiel to bear the iniquity of Israel by laying on his left side for 390 days. He is to stay on his side, not to turn; next, he is to lay on his right side 40 days, for the iniquity of Judah. Water and barley cakes, baked over human dung, sufficient to sustain him, are to be provided. Ezekiel takes issue with the human dung, so God lets him bake his cakes over cow dung, which is often used as a fuel in that region. The Bible does not say that Ezekiel carried out this order. If he did, I wonder how he handled going to the bathroom. Imagine the 430 days of human waste Ezekiel would have generated!

Of course, that pales in comparison with the mountains of dung and the sea of urine that two of each animal would generate in a year on a literal ark of Noah's. Perhaps there is no better example of intellectual dishonesty than believing the Bible story about the ark to be true – except possibly the foolish belief in a 6,000-year-old earth. Earth has millions of species of animals. The size of the ark described in the Bible would accommodate only a tiny fraction of two of each animal – seven each of the kosher ones – plus a year's supply of food. There would be plenty of water to drink, but how would the animals get to it? Not to mention the fact that Noah's family of eight people – among other impossible problems than those of feeding and watering – would require several lifetimes to load and unload their cargo. Arctic animals would be especially time-consuming. Not that they matter, since the ark would be more than filled from a local geography. Curiously, creatures that live in the water are never addressed.

Believers assume they simply survived in the flood waters; however, this is contrary to Genesis' story in which God repeatedly says He will destroy all flesh, excepting only the occupants of the ark. Besides, if God struck down all but two of each water creature, why not do the same to land creatures, plus save Noah's family? Then, all that water and the ark would not be necessary.

Anyone can pick and choose biblical verses to defend various points of view. Debates may ensue about who has the right interpretation. Value judgment as to how one's understanding relates to reality in the present day is the only means of obtaining progressive or useful insight that may be acted upon.

From the New Testament, ponder the tremendous implication of Jesus' new commandment in John 13:34-35 in which he tells his disciples to love one another as he has loved them and by doing so all men shall know that they are disciples of Jesus. So, anyone who loves other human beings to the best of his ability is a disciple of Jesus. Religious belief or theological understanding are not a part of this teaching. Does not this say that a Jew, Muslim, Hindu, Buddhist or even an atheist can be a disciple of Jesus? The proof can be seen in living reality by the expression of love, one to another.

Luke 14:26 presents a giant contradiction to this new commandment in John. Jesus says, "Whoever comes to me and does not hate father and mother, wife and children, brothers and sisters, yes, and even life itself, cannot be my disciple." Matthew 10:37 has a similar, but milder version of this verse. What are we to think of Jesus' saying such a thing? The *King James Study Bible* (KJSB) justifies this verse as "vivid hyperbole, meaning that one must love Jesus even more than one's own immediate family;" then gives Matthew 10:37 for another use of the figure.

In my mind, this is a destructive explanation for biblical reliability. Hyperbole, defined by my Webster Dictionary, is: "extravagant exaggeration used as a figure of speech." In other words, these experts are saying that Jesus used vivid, extravagant exaggeration to make his point. He simply meant that one must love Jesus more than his own family. In reality, if that explanation is accepted, what is to prevent applying this meaning to any other difficult saying of Jesus, his apostles, or any other troubling biblical saying? Vivid hyperbole seems like a realistic explanation for dead saints coming out of their graves and going into Jerusalem, as discussed previously.

The verse after Luke 14:26 might provide some insight into this troubling saying of Jesus. Luke 14:27 and 9:23 – like the two verses in Mark, as well as two in Matthew – have Jesus saying to take up the cross and follow Him in order to be His disciple. The problem is these six verses are talking about the cross before there has been any mention of a crucifixion. The indication is that many years later while writing their gospels, Luke and Matthew probably using Mark as their source, all made the mistake of having Jesus refer to the cross before anyone would have known its meaning. If the editors of these three gospels overlooked so simple a mistake, then it is reasonable to assume that Luke in 14:26 – as well as Matthew in his verse – unintentionally misquoted Jesus. Consider the dramatic difference the term "not" makes in Luke's version. Leave it out and "does not hate" becomes "does hate." Whoever does hate their life or family members cannot be Jesus' disciple sounds a lot more in synch with Jesus' two greatest commands, as well as John's so-named new commandment.

Intellectual honesty tends to coordinate sayings and events with reality. Much of what the Old Testament prophets declare is repetitious, confusing and of little value for present day application. Many of their sayings do not resonate with an intelligent God of love. Although they all claim the Lord said thus and so, they give ample reasons for doubt. Consider Jeremiah 51:44. God is saying that he will punish Bel in Babylon and make him disgorge what he has swallowed. Bel is the chief god of the Babylonians. Since Bel's reality is that of an idol or statue, how is it punished? Jeremiah may have thought he was speaking for God, but I don't. Surely God would know Bel was not a real being or god, but apparently Jeremiah thought otherwise.

Recall that the Hebrews gave us the Old Testament, which is vague about an afterlife. For example, in Daniel 12:2 we find: "And many of them that sleep in the dust of the earth shall awake, some to everlasting life and some to shame and everlasting contempt;" and Hosea 13:14 reads: "I will ransom them from the power of the grave; I will redeem them from death . . .". At least the *King James* and *Jewish Bible* have God saying to Israel that He will redeem them from death. The *New Revised Standard Version* has God putting it as a question: shall I redeem them from death? Neither Daniel nor Hosea say that this applies to everybody. Both do indicate an afterlife for at least some people. This verse of Daniel not only reveals a raising of the good and bad, but also is the only Old Testament passage that has the dead returning to an everlasting life.

However, Ecclesiastes 9:5-6 and 9:10 imply that the dead never ever again experience anything. The writer of Ecclesiastes seems confused as he ends his text saying that God will judge every deed of every person, whether good or bad. The writer had already ventured this opinion earlier in Ecclesiastes. Of course, he may have thought that all reward or punishment occurred during one's lifetime. Judaism in general takes the position that we should live morally in the fashion of loving God and neighbor – not for reward in the next life, but doing the right thing in this life. No reward or punishment is predicted after physical death. That one's soul survives death is an accepted teaching. As Ecclesiastes 12:7 puts it, the soul's duty is to return to God from which it came. It should be noted that today non-Orthodox Jews have a wide variety of beliefs on subjects like this.

It is also thought that Jews, with the exception of the gospel of Luke and his Book of Acts, authored the New Testament. Both the Gospel of Luke and the Book of Acts were strongly influenced by Paul who was a Jew. Some argue that Mark was a gentile. Probably one quarter or more of the New Testament is based on passages, events or language from the Old Testament! New Testament writers clearly looked to the Old Testament for much of their information. Their acceptance of Jesus as the Messiah, whom Jews had long expected, necessitated a change from their thinking of a military king to conquer Israel's enemies to a passive king with a spiritual kingdom who would reward them in the next life. Mixing the new with the old justified the fact of the authors' portrayal of events and sayings that were not factual. An example is Matthew's and Luke's need for genealogies to show Jesus' descent from David. Most of their lineage was taken from the Old Testament, but here Matthew and Luke were not copying from a common source for all their information, thus wound up with conflict. This does not mean that the New Testament is fiction. Like the Old Testament, much of its content contains truth that has been compromised by the writer's passion as well as their reliance on second-hand information that was erroneous. Why are there so many compromises in both Testaments?

Perhaps a large factor in Old Testament contradictions is that different stories about similar circumstances, written by different people, have been combined into one story. Why would anyone do that instead of choosing one version over the other? It was part of the reunification process around the time of the rebuilding of the first temple. Previously, the Hebrews had been divided into two kingdoms – Israel and Judah. Each side had different authorities that composed conflicting stories. The editor or editors that compiled the Holy Scriptures during this period had to use material from both sides in order to satisfy differing religious instruction. Richard Elliott Friedman's *Who Wrote the Bible?* is an excellent, understandable book on this ancient subject.

Many times I have read or heard comments about how archaeology and history have proved the Bible accurate. Some take this statement to mean that science has proven the Bible to be true. Thus, God's word is always dependable. However, most books of fiction contain some actual people, places or events that can be confirmed by archaeology and history. Yet the stories and most characters remain pure fiction.

There is no archaeological or historical evidence that confirms the Bible's story about the Israelites ever being slaves in Egypt or that the Exodus ever happened. This story is the foundation of the Jewish religion and in the sense that Christianity branched from Judaism, that is also the basis of the Christian religion. Of course, lack of any confirming evidence is not proof that the story is untrue. Even if actual history, this would not mean that all the Bible story is factual.

I remember a discussion I once had with a literalist Bible believer who was adamant that Isaiah 40:22 in mentioning the circle of the earth scientifically proved God was talking to Isaiah because everyone thought the earth was flat during Isaiah's time. I disagreed, saying that some people saw a round sun and round moon and possibly thought the earth was shaped that way. Bible literalists embrace science if it tends to validate what they already believe. Many are just as quick to reject well-documented science if it disagrees.

A major factor in New Testament sayings is the delay of many years between Jesus' life and the actual writing down of His story. Consider that at least half of the New Testament's text is generally credited to Luke and Paul, neither of whom ever met the Person of Jesus. The indication is that much of what we read today is based on, at best, second-hand information and is dependent on translations from other languages as well as numerous human copiers who wrote by hand.

My point has been sufficiently made as to why the Bible may not be the best guide to post-death experience. While the Old Testament is scant about the hereafter, the New Testament leaves little doubt about an afterlife that will reward the good and punish the bad. Most of Christianity has traditionally seen life after death as plain and simple. Jesus must be accepted as one's savior in order to have eternal life in heaven with God and the angels. Everybody else is destined to an eternal hell of fire. Many see hell as the kingdom of the devil, known as Satan or Lucifer, even though the name Lucifer appears only once in older Bibles and not at all in modern ones. Catholicism includes a place or state of temporary punishment that is called purgatory. Purgatory is for people who were not too bad during their lifetime and with additional purification they can still go to heaven. Ultimately, everybody spends eternity either in heaven or in hell. A favorite tool of theologians has been the fear of the horrors of hell in getting converts to Christianity. In modern times some pastors – including Billy Graham – have moved away from a hell of burning in favor of hell as separation from God. Bible support can be found in 2 Thessalonians 1:8-9, where it says that those who do not obey the gospel of Jesus will suffer the punishment of eternal destruction, separated from the Lord.

Just as most theologians have given us little detail on exactly what the saved will be doing in heaven for all eternity, I'm not aware of what the post-death experience, if any, will be for those separated from God. Only the ones holding to a fire and brimstone hell know specifically what is in store for its occupants.

Ponder the Bible's use of the term hell. The *King James Bible* (KJ) mentions hell 31 times in the Old Testament, but only Deuteronomy 32:22 uses the word fire in the same verse. The New Testament has 23 references to hell. Some are repeated parallel passages. Several verses also contain the word fire. One of these, Revelation 20:14, personifies death and hell that are cast into a lake of fire.

The much more modern *New Revised Standard Version of the Bible* (NRSV), like an English translation of the *Jewish Bible*, does not contain the word hell in the Old Testament. Where the KJ has hell, the NRSV prefers the Jewish word *sheol*, generally translated the grave. The Jewish Bible uses *sheol* in all but two passages where it says grave once and netherworld once. Remember, the Jewish Bible does not include the New Testament. The NRSV substitutes the Greek word *hades* for ten usages of the word hell in the KJ New Testament. The NRSV and KJ agree on the remaining thirteen uses of the word hell. The Old Testament authors use the word 'fire' more than 450 times, yet do not appear to have had any concept of an afterlife punishment of a fiery hell as a place where sinners will have to spend eternity. The New Testament has some rather odd verses about hell and fire. In Matthew 5:22 Jesus says if you call someone a fool, you will be liable to the hell of fire. In Matthew 18:8-9 Jesus says if one of your hands, feet or eyes causes you to stumble, tear it off and throw it away, saying it is better to enter life with one member than keep two members and to be thrown into the hell of fire. Verse 8 uses the term eternal fire. Mark 9:43-47 is a more or less a repeat of Matthew 18:8-9. Another New Testament passage that has the words fire and hell is James 3:6. Here, the tongue is called a fire, a world of iniquity, itself set on fire by hell. Surely none of these strange passages support a universal punishment of sinners by an eternal fiery hell. The New Testament mentions everlasting or eternal fire. Matthew 13:40-42 and 49-50 specifically say that at the end of the age, evildoers will be thrown into the furnace of fire, while 13:43 says the righteous will shine like the sun in the Kingdom of their Father. Perhaps Matthew should have phrased that differently, for in order to shine like the sun, one would have to burn like the sun. In any case, the relevant point is that nowhere in the Bible does it say a hell of fire is the place where all the unsaved will spend eternity. Certainly, if that was the case, a divinely inspired Bible would have made that point perfectly clear in both the Old and New Testaments.

As to the term heaven, the word is used some 550 times in the Bible, about 50 more times in the Old Testament than New Testament. In addition, the plural term heavens is used over 130 times, mostly, in the Old Testament with the New

Testament having only 19 uses. To my knowledge, there is no verse in the Old Testament that justifies an eternal life in heaven for the good guys. If we disregard Ecclesiastes, we may allow that Daniel 12:2 indicates everlasting life for some people. But it says nothing about where this life will take place.

The nearest the New Testament gets is Matthew 5:12 or the parallel of Luke 6:23 in which Jesus is saying to rejoice and be glad, for your reward is great in heaven. This reward is addressed to those who endure persecution for Jesus' sake. The New Testament refers to eternal or everlasting life over thirty times – the majority being in the gospel of John – but nowhere does it say heaven is where this life occurs. Consider: where is heaven located? In the ignorance of the biblical authors' time, they thought heaven was simply in the sky, just like they thought stars were small lights that could fall to earth or act like a moving spotlight to lead the wise men to Jesus. Science has enlightened us on stars, but has been unable to locate heaven. We can only posit heaven and the sky as synonymous. Some Christian denominations, such as Mormons and Jehovah Witnesses, do get more specific about the next life. Notwithstanding that, many mainline Christians reject both sects as Christians.

Before moving on to some nonmainstream ideas, John 13:34-35 should be revisited. An Evangelical interpretation might be that Jesus meant that his disciple must love another enough to die on the cross. This twist demonstrates that much Christian theology depends on making the evidence fit a preconceived belief. John has Jesus' saying occurring before anyone would know about the epic cross.

3 MORMONS AND JEHOVAH WITNESSES

Mormons consider the Bible to be Holy Scripture alongside the *Book of Mormon*, the *Doctrine and Covenants* and the *Pearl of Great Price*. All three are mainly the work of Joseph Smith, Jr., based on direct, divine revelation that he supposedly received. During the second quarter of the nineteenth century, Joseph Smith founded the Mormon church, which is best known as the Church of Jesus Christ of Latter Day Saints. There are other, lesser-known independent Mormon denominations. A revealing read is that of David Persuitte's second edition of *Joseph Smith and the Origins of the Book of Mormon*. There is much information available that questions the credibility of Joseph Smith and his teachings. What I like about Persuitte's book is that it is not tainted by any preconceived religious perspective. His text gives ample evidence for rejecting Joseph Smith and his doctrines as being commissioned by God, which is the Mormon church's position. Even if Smith's claim of direct divine help cannot be trusted and deceit was involved, his views are at least speculation and imagination. Both of the latter attributes have played major roles in every existing religion, especially concerning the afterlife. That is the rationale for exploring Mormon post-death concepts. Joseph Smith, Jr. and every head of the Mormon church since then is considered a prophet, hence adjustments and additions have occurred to Mormon teaching. For example, section 137 and section 138 have been added to the *Doctrine and Covenants* in the late 1970s based on claimed revelations. Section 137 reverses the former teaching of not allowing black men to hold the priesthood. Many non-Mormons see this as a convenient revelation caused by social pressure from the civil rights movement. Section 138 concerns the spirit world.

A brief Mormon overview concerning the next life goes something like this: God was born on another planet and was like man is today. Based on the *Doctrine and* Covenants 130:22, the Mormon church teaches that God the Father and His Son Jesus Christ actually appeared to Joseph Smith in 1820. Smith revealed that the Father and the Son each have "a body of flesh and bones as tangible as man's" (website of the Mormon church: www.lds.org, March 20, 2007) – notwithstanding that Smith was age fourteen at the time, the Mormon church accepts his claim as truth. Revealingly, this triggers the thought about my own age fourteen experience of trees becoming alien monsters due to my mind being overstimulated by a movie.

Then, after originally coming into existence with man's limitations, God evolved to his present almighty state, but he is still subject to certain fixed laws of the universe. He, together with a co-creator, divine mother were the parents of spirits, of whom Jesus was the first-born. These spirits eventually became humans. Man has the potential of becoming godlike and, ultimately, of ruling his own planet. When man reaches God status, he and his then-divine wife will produce spirit offspring to populate their planet. A famous quote from the Bible justifies all this: "God created humankind in his image" (Genesis 1:27). Special ceremonies are performed in Mormon temples to seal marriage forever.

Biblical support is found in 1 Corinthians 11:11; "In the Lord, woman is not independent of man or man independent of woman." Not only does this sealing bond spouses to each other, but also bonds children to parents. Mormons place great emphasis on genealogies because it is possible to include every ancestor, including those not in one's direct chain of descent, into a huge eternal family. There is a special ceremony in the Mormon church for the dead so they may still receive the ultimate reward. Biblical authority is inferred for this sealing power from Matthew 16:19 where Jesus is saying that he is giving Peter the keys of the kingdom of heaven, so whatever Peter binds on earth will be bound in heaven. Also, whatever he loosens on earth will be loosened in heaven. Mormons attach the same meaning to the word bind as they do to the word seal. Interestingly, the Catholic Church sees this verse, together with Matthew 16:18 as the justification for establishment of the Papacy. Peter is considered to be the first Pope. How did the Mormon church get its binding authority? Joseph Smith said he received it from the prophet Elijah. Joseph Smith reported that other, resurrected Biblical personalities appeared to him that include Moses, Elias, John the Baptist and some of the original twelve Apostles. Did Elijah come back to earth the way he left – in a whirlwind?

Just as the Papacy has been passed on from one pope to another, across the centuries for 2,000 years, Mormon prophets, for less than a couple of hundred years, have passed their sealing authority in the same way. Let's return to the concept of the Mormon hereafter.

According to Mormon belief, after death everyone returns to his pre-mortal spirit state to await resurrection when Jesus and his apostles will do the judging on judgment day. The spirit world consists of spirit paradise and spirit prison. Devout Mormons believe that the good guys will inhabit spirit paradise, while spirit prison is for the wicked who died in their sins. While the good await judgment day, they socialize, continue to gain knowledge, and serve God in various ways. Those in spirit prison – Mormon purgatory – still get the chance to repent of their sins. The worse one's sins, the longer the stay in prison. Mortal Mormons – through the special rituals for the dead performed in the Mormon church – can help those spirits in prison qualify for a better eternity on judgment day. Oddly, only a mortal with a physical body can effectively perform the rituals for the dead. According to Mormon thinking, at judgment everybody will be bodily resurrected and depending on merit and repentance be eternally assigned to one of three heavens. The Bible mentions John's vision of a first heaven that passes away (Revelation 21:1) and a third heaven that Paul seems to think is paradise (2 Corinthians 12:2-4). Thus, there is logically a second heaven.

The lowest heaven – the telestial – will be the abode of unrepentant sinners that rejected the Gospel of Jesus even in the Spirit world: adulterers, liars, murderers, rapists and others who died in their sins.

The second heaven – the terrestrial – is the eternal home of good people who more or less did not faithfully accept Mormon teachings. Occupants of the first two heavens will be limited in their eternal progress – the first more so than the second – and will live forever without family relationships and with the knowledge that they will never qualify for God status. To a degree, their hell is eternal existence.

Only certain folks can obtain the highest heaven – the celestial. The celestial is reserved for faithful Mormons, for those who never heard of the Mormon gospel, but who would have fully accepted it if they had, and for all children who died before reaching eight years of age. God himself is said to live in the celestial kingdom. Here, the inhabitants may work and progress through the celestial's own multi-levels to the ultimate prize of becoming Gods.

Also according to Mormon thinking, there is an eternal hell for the most evil of beings. This includes the devil with his angels and the sons of perdition, defined as those who ultimately rejected the gospel after completely understanding and accepting it.

There is some confusion about Mormon eternal hell, likely caused by the addition of section 138 to the *Doctrine and Covenants*. One of my references, *Mormonism for Dummies*, by Jana Riess, Ph.D., and Christopher Kimball Bigelow, calls it outer darkness, best described as the complete absence of light and warmth. Wikipedia, the free encyclopedia on the internet, gives two uses of Mormon outer darkness. One is Scriptural use per the *Book of Mormon*. Alma 40:13, contained within this source, tells of those that chose evil works rather than good and are cast into outer darkness. Alma 40:14 reveals that they stay there until their resurrection. Modern Latter Day Saints view this as spirit prison. The second most common use of outer darkness by present Latter Day Saints sees it as an eternal state of punishment devoid of any light. Any references about hell-fire are thought to be figurative of the sufferings endured by those willfully disobeying God.

A dark and cold hell is in conflict with the Bible and with Mormonism's own accepted scripture. *The Doctrine and Covenants* 76:36, referring to the sons of perdition, says "these are they who shall go away into the lake of fire and brimstone, with the devil and his angels." *D and C* 76:44, again referring to the sons of perdition, says "wherefore he saves all except them – they shall go away into everlasting punishment, . . . and the fire is not quenched, which is their torment." The terms "fire and brimstone" and "the fire is not quenched" specifically followed by "which is their torment," plainly indicate that when Joseph Smith wrote this, he meant actual fire and was making no figurative illusion to dark and cold.

The New Testament in Matthew 13:42 and 13:50 says that evildoers will be thrown into the furnace of fire. While in Matthew 25:41 Jesus will say to the accursed, "Depart from me, into the eternal fire prepared for the devil and his angels." None of these three verses give any indication that fire was in any way figuratively meant to mean its opposite. In fact, the term 'furnace of fire' is clear confirmation of actual fire.

In the above may be a clue as to how questionable teachers really get their revelations. An ambiguous saying from the Bible, other sacred scripture or other information including scientific information, creates an idea that – when the human mind operates naturally – the teacher's speculation and imagination builds on. Mormon thinking on outer darkness plainly originated in the Book of Matthew's unexplained meaning for its three uses of the term. While science has methods to adjust error toward truth, its tools do not work with the purely supernatural: to date, science has been unable to confirm anything about the supernatural; however, it has been able to deny some religious beliefs.

Mormonism's ongoing chain of prophets – like Catholicism's much longer chain of popes – must limit their ideas to an acceptable blend with their predecessors. If not, then schism usually results in new, independent denominations that profess the same faith, but with different twists. On the other hand, if the church leaders become too dogmatic and refuse any change to their tradition – even though the times or human use dictate a need to change – then schism also results in new sects. The result may be also that the faithful simply ignore some of the traditional rules.

According to the 2001 edition of the *World Christian Encyclopedia*, published by Oxford University Press, there are no less than 33,830 Christian denominations worldwide. Every one of them accept the Bible as Sacred Scripture, although I believe a tiny few are discarding the Old Testament to look only to the New Testament. Naturally, a vast number of twists in interpretation of various passages accommodate so many denominations. One thing this should tell us is that the Bible is not a consistent, clearly written book of instructions from God. In Christianity alone we have some different 34,000 churches as evidence. I am confident that if God ever intended to communicate with humankind or reveal His will mainly from a book, He would have inspired a vastly improved Bible. The same holds true for every existing book of so-called Holy Scriptures. Consider: when we credit God as the Bible's real author, we are also saying He was a very poor writer in clearly conveying so many important points, even that of eternal life for His creatures.

Before leaving Mormonism, it should be noted that the Bible is quoted to support its theology, as is common to Christianity in general. Yet, as seen by the example of a cold hell, the Bible may deny some of its teaching. Another telling example concerns Joseph Smith's revelation that God has a body of flesh and bones. The Mormon church's website, cited previously, lists some Bible verses as evidence: two of these, Genesis 32:30 and Exodus 33:11, have Jacob seeing God "face to face" and God speaking to Moses "face to face." It would seem, then, God must have a human-type face. However, in the same chapter that Moses is "face to face" with God, another verse disputes that Jacob, Moses, nor Joseph Smith ever saw God. In Exodus 33:20 God tells Moses, "No one shall see me and live." Since Jacob, Moses and Joseph Smith all lived for many years after supposedly seeing God, then certainly one, maybe two, or possibly all three of these verses are untrue. Additionally, Exodus 24:10-11 states that Moses as well as other Israelites saw God. John 1:18 and 1 John 4:12 give New Testament authority to the fact that no one has ever seen God. As Joseph Smith's time was some 1800 years later, the latter two verses would not be applicable to him. In any case, we have at least three Scripture passages declaring that humans saw God and three that disagree.

There are other New Testament verses that only compound this confusion. In John 6:46 Jesus, referring to himself, says to a party of Jews, "Not that anyone has seen the Father except the one who is from God." In John 14:9 Jesus responds to Philip's request to show us the Father by saying, "Whoever has seen me has seen the Father." 1 Timothy 6:16 complicates more than it clarifies, in addressing the King of Kings and Lord of Lords, which appears to mean Jesus, by saying, "It is he alone who has immortality and dwells in unapproachable light, whom no one has seen or can see."

It is revealing to see how the *King James Study Bible* deals with this contradictory information. Its study note on John 1:18 explains that sometimes people in the Old Testament are said to have seen God, but also that no one can see God and live. Then, pure speculation takes over in saying that since no human can see God as he really is, "those who saw

God saw him in a form he took on himself temporarily for the occasion." Then we are told that those events are known as "Christophanies" or Old Testament appearances of Jesus in human form. Ponder this, if one saw God in any form, would not that form still be God?

I suppose no amount of evidence would change the thinking of those who believe the Bible to be "God's infallible word to humanity," which is the way the introduction to the *King James Study Bible* describes the belief of its scholars. Rather than admit that some passages may not be true, they resort to creative imagination and feel free to speak for God and explain his actions. The above "Christophanies" are a case in point. Here, God and Jesus are viewed as equals.

Jehovah's Witnesses' theology would disagree. While they accept Jesus as the first being whom God created – and who became the Archangel Michael – they do not consider Jesus to be God's equal. Like Catholics, Mormons and others, the Jehovah Witnesses consider their organization to be God's kingdom on earth; the latter even call their churches "Kingdom Hall." Generally, Jehovah Witnesses (JWs) view the devil as controlling all churches except their own.

JWs' founder was Charles Taze Russell, a businessman and Bible student who became involved in the publication of religious material. In 1879 he began a magazine that evolved into the present Watchtower magazine, the official publication of this denomination.

During the last quarter of the nineteenth century Russell incorporated "Zion's Watchtower Tract Society" for religious purposes. In 1896 the name changed to "Watchtower Bible and Tract Society." Russell died in 1916. In 1931, his successor, Joseph F. Rutherford, changed the name of the organization to "Jehovah's Witnesses." Under the legal name of "Watchtower and Bible Tract Society," the entity continues to distribute a tremendous amount of religious literature.

JWs got their name from Isaiah 43:10 and 43:12. But in order to find the name "Jehovah" in those verses, one must reference the JWs' own version of the Bible, *New World Translation of the Holy Scriptures*, first published in the 1950s in multiple volumes, then, as one book in the 1960s. The word "Jehovah" is a mistranslation or misspelling that first appeared in the eleventh century as a form of the Hebrew name for Israel's God Yahweh. The sixteenth century translation of the Bible in English by William Tyndale included the name Jehovah. Originally, Jews considered God's name too holy to even pronounce, thus designated it with four letters for which the English equivalent is Y H W H or J H V H. Due to mixing these consonants with vowels attached to another divine name, Adonai, the erroneous "Jehovah" appears in some Bibles. While the *King James* version uses "Jehovah" seven times, it does not do so in Isaiah 43:10 or 43:12, where it renders, instead, "Ye are my witnesses, saith the Lord." Most of the time – but not always – the JWs' Bible uses the word "Jehovah" to replace the word "Lord." Jehovah God, Lord Jehovah and God are also used in the JW Bible. Although the name Jehovah is now commonly defined as a name of God, it was used only once in a known Hebrew publication. Hebrew scholars prefer the name Yahweh, which was the result of adding vowels to the original four consonants that designated God.

My copy of *New World Translation of the Holy Scriptures* says that 114,590,000 copies have been printed. Multiply this by the thousands of usages of the word "Jehovah" in each copy, and we find that the word "Jehovah" must qualify for the *Guinness Book of Records* as the single most repeated word based on a misspelling of all time. Curiously, as there must now be over 120 million JWs' Bibles that have been printed, and with an estimated six to seven million active JWs members – the majority reside outside the United States – why do they need so many of their own Bibles, particularly when they teach that it is OK to use other Bibles?

In addition to the Bible, JWs considered Charles T. Russell's *Studies in the Scriptures* as essential text. A series of seven volumes, the first six were published over a period from 1889 to 1904. The seventh was published in 1917, after Russell's death. It was promoted as his posthumous work. Later, it was found that the seventh volume was actually the work of two Russell associates and had been edited by Russell's successor Joseph Rutherford. Due to this deception, but mainly to the Society's changing prophecies about the date of Jesus' second coming, all seven volumes were eventually withdrawn from circulation. The seventh volume is titled the *Finished Mysteries*. It includes a detailed interpretation of the Book of Revelation.

Only the Watchtower and Bible Tract Societies' interpretation of any Holy Scripture is considered by JWs to be accurate. JW members are encouraged to read literature that is published only by the Watchtower and Bible Tract Society. The Society asserts firm control over the thoughts and actions of its members. The fact of not following the Society's firm rules will result in excommunication of the offending member, who is then avoided by faithful congregants, except in cases of business or their own family household situations. It is possible for the excommunicated to be reinstated to the congregation.

With this background, l will explore the afterlife teachings of JWs who say there is no soul that is separate from the body. The soul is simply the life-animating energy of the body and dies when the body dies. All consciousness ceases at death. According to JWs, the faithful dead await resurrection from the grave and with a new body will inhabit the new earth that will be paradise. Based on Revelation 7 and Revelation 14, a group of 144,000 resurrected people are of special status and will be redeemed from the grave to live in heaven with God. This special group will become pure spirits, while those on earth have physical bodies. The spirit group with God will rule over those inhabiting the new paradise on earth. Only loyal JWs will survive the grave. The unresurrected never regain any consciousness; thus, for most folks the grave is eternal hell. There is no fiery burning for Jehovah Witnesses.

JW and Watchtower literature depends mainly on their interpretation of biblical verses to justify their teachings. Yet, if approached with minimal preconceived prejudice, the Bible may defeat some teachings. A good example is the special class of 144,000 that receive the ultimate reward in the hereafter. In the United States, the KJ was the Bible of choice when Russell set down the importance of this special class. What does the KJ tell us? "And there were sealed 144,000 of all the tribes of the children of Israel" (Revelation 7:4). Verses 7:5 through 7:8 go on to name the twelve tribes of Israel with 12,000 of the sealed coming from each tribe. Revelation 14:4 refers to the 144,000, saying "These are they which were not defiled with women, for they are virgins." Although the Book of Revelation is rampant with bizarre language, these quotes about the 144,000 are quite clear. They will be Jews who are virgins. The wording leaves little doubt that these virgins are males. The KJ study note on 14:4 says that the concept of being not defiled with women could be a symbolic description for those believers that did not have defiling relationships with the pagan world system or could mean the 144,000 are only males. Accepting the symbolic explanation as defiling relationships with the pagan world is quite farfetched, since the verse plainly names women as the would-be cause of defilement.

The KJ study note on Revelation 7:4 comments that the 144,000 must be actual Jews even though others take the passage as symbolic of faithful believers who live during the tribulation period. In my thinking, this symbolic view is an unacceptable stretch of imagination. In any case, if you have to be a Jewish man that is a virgin to make it to heaven and live with God, no women and few men will have a chance to qualify. The best they can hope for is eternal life on the new earth. This fact creates a real problem for JWs' theology. Since their teachings include that only faithful JWs will be resurrected, they better concentrate their considerable door-to-door missionary techniques on young Jewish men that have not had sex and those that become JWs must then stay virgins.

It gets more complicated than this, as the Bible requires that these Jews be equally descended from each of the twelve tribes of Israel. Odds do not appear to favor 144,000 JWs ever getting to heaven. Of course, the Watchtower and Bible Tract Societies' teachings regarding the 144,000 keep changing. In the past they taught that all 144,000 were sealed in 1914.

At that time the Society's theology had to make an adjustment to compensate for its failed prophecy that Jesus would return in 1914 to begin the end times. The Watchtower Society taught that Jesus did return in 1914, but stayed invisible to most folks. He did begin the end times and seal the 144,000. Later, the 1914 date for the sealed was revised at least once before being changed again to 1931. Several times the Watchtower Society has adjusted its teachings about Jesus and the end times. These changes were necessitated because of the Society's previous erroneous predictions.

Due to this confusion, the understanding on the sealing of the 144,000 has been refined. In the May 1, 2007 edition of the Watchtower magazine, on page 30, a reader asks, "When does the calling of Christians to a heavenly hope cease?" The first sentence of the response is that the Bible does not reveal a precise answer to that question. Then, over a full page is devoted to a rambling, confusing answer that references over twenty Biblical passages. In my opinion most of these passages have no relation to the "anointed Christians," as the Watchtower prefers to call them. In any case, its answer is that a specific date cannot be set for when the calling of Christians to the heavenly hope ends. Note that Revelation's 144,000 Jews have become, in the reader's question, "Christians to a heavenly hope," and, in the Watchtower's view, "anointed Christians."

By strong reliance on Revelation's reference to this special group, Charles Taze Russell himself would be excluded as one of the 144,000. Intellectual dishonesty by ignoring what the verses actually say is the only technique to conclude otherwise. Belief or faith about what happens in the next life – whether right or wrong – is harmless enough, but when that faith requires specific action in this life the result may be beneficial to society. However, narrow-minded adherence to an interpretation of Sacred Scripture or religious authority that one accepts as an inflexible mandate can lead to disaster.

JWs beliefs present some plain examples. Faithful JWs reject blood transfusions because Genesis 9:4 and Leviticus 17:12 and 14 say not to eat blood. Also, Acts 15:29 instructs to abstain from blood. JWs consider injecting blood into blood vessels to be the same as eating it. Adults and children have died because of JWs' rejection of proper medical treatment that required transfusions. Today, in the case of children, most medical centers would appeal to the courts to authorize proper treatment over the objection of parents. Such parents may be charged with child abuse. Freedom of religion is their sole defense.

JWs also reject serving in the military. Why? Because they believe that if civil law is in conflict with God's law, that God's law is to be followed. They do not believe that God has ordered men into battle since the days of ancient Israel. This parallels some Islamic thought that the best government is a theocracy: rule should be by God's law, without separation of church and state. Many evangelical Christians appear to prefer a theocracy. There is a difference between the three religious views: JWs are awaiting God to call them back to battle; Muslims look to Mohammed's example of *jihad* – a holy war against unbelievers – any time circumstances are interpreted as appropriate; Evangelicals seem to think that God has continuously called Christians to battle the wicked, even militarily, if necessary.

I am not suggesting that the JWs' refusal to go to war based on civil need is a disaster. But consider the consequence if the vast majority of US citizens accepted the JWs' inflexible mandate. Without a strong military, how long would the US survive as an independent democracy? Inflexible mandates in religion or in the secular world may, in the long run, be disastrous. History should reveal that a theocracy governing any nation will approximate the same result as nations run by dictators. The only real difference is a dictatorship mainly has one individual wielding absolute power based on personal preference, while a theocracy may have a chosen few in absolute control. Of course, the theocrats have got their instructions from God, and, regrettably, these instructions depend on their accepted interpretation relating to their one, true religion.

Experience is our greatest teacher; it plainly shows the danger of a theocracy as is so visible today in some Muslims' actions. In the ancient past, the Hebraic theocracy instituted the horror of death by stoning for such things as working on the Sabbath, being a disobedient child, being deemed a heretic, and, of course, for adultery – which was severely slanted toward punishing women since men could have all the wives they could support. The ancient Catholic (universal) Church, while only a limited theocracy, increased its revolting mandates in direct proportion to the amount of civil power it obtained, as evidenced by the Crusades, the Inquisition and the burning of heretics at the stake.

A nation utilizing a justice-minded secular government is the only one that produces democracy for its people. We need to rectify a huge mistake that many make about their understanding of the secular. Secular is defined as not related or concerned with religion. This does not mean that it opposes religion, in fact, in a democratic, secular government like that of the United States, then it allows the practice of any religion that any individual or group wants, provided one does not break civil laws that were legislated to benefit all people – religious as well as nonreligious. In spite of the many claims of religionists, this nation was not founded on Christian principles, but on secular ones. The separation of church and state allows Christians as well other faiths to have any holy books, authorities and beliefs that they want as long as they do not violate the civil laws of the land. Christian principles would require the Bible as the primary holy book and that all citizens become adherents to Christian teachings – notwithstanding the confusion of just which Christian denominations really teach the truth. Of course, many secular principles parallel Christian as well as other religious views in issues such as prohibitions against murder, violence, theft, and so forth.

As has already been demonstrated God and the Bible may be used by devotees to support what they prefer to believe. Reality shows us this method does not always relate to truth. Consider the popular patriotic saying, "God bless America." Isn't that a little selfish? Why should God bless us and not the rest of the world? An often-repeated answer is, God blesses us because we are a Christian nation. Often the addendum is given that the blessing may soon stop if all the abortions, homosexuality, pornography, and the like, are allowed to continue. Interestingly, about the time I wrote this, I saw a television interview by a journalist with the late Reverend Jerry Falwell, who again reminded us God may remove His protection from the United States that He has given in the past because of abortions and homosexuality. Many evangelicals agree.

If Falwell is correct, I have to wonder why God protected this nation during all those years in which slavery was allowed or discrimination against minorities and women that exist in lesser degrees to this day. Remember, it was civil law and its enforcement that abolished slavery in spite of many quoting from the Bible in favor of slavery. That does not mean there were no individual Christians or other religionists who historically opposed slavery. Similar to Martin Luther King, as an individual Christian minister leading the charge against racial discrimination in his day, some of the faithful of the past did their part to oppose slavery. The point being: Christianity as an institution never devoted the effort against slavery or racial discrimination that it now does to abortion and homosexuality. Secular law protects minorities and women, while numerous religious organizations continue their prejudice of females. Falwell and company only became super-inspired against abortion and homosexuality when civil law offered the protection of making each legal. Perhaps Falwell and associates confused their own inspired position as that of God. This is not meant to promote a position either for or against embryonic stage abortion. However, after the first few weeks and particularly partial birth abortion, except in extremely rare circumstances, appears very wrong.

I think it again appropriate to state my purpose is not to insult anyone's biblical or religious beliefs. The Bible plainly contradicts itself in many instances. And many religious figures use the pulpit to promote their own agenda while presenting it as that of God. Opposite conclusions can be supported by different biblical sayings.

Was President G. W. Bush's famous saying, "You are either with us or against us," inspired by the Bible? He said this in November of 2001 in an effort to gain support from other nations for his version on how the war against terrorism should be conducted. Most nations, while agreeing Saddam Hussein should go, did not agree that war with Iraq was the best way to fight terrorism. On hindsight, it seems the majority was right and Bush was wrong. Will history tell a different story? What does the Bible have to do with this? Consider Mark 9:40: "Whoever is not against us, is for us." Then, Luke 11:23 has a similar saying. The central point is that even true inspiration from the Bible, like that of other sources, does not always direct one to the right path.

This in no way is meant to discourage believers from searching the Bible for inspiration. Just don't lose sight of reality and common sense. Before acting on any inspiration, be sure it is the right thing to do based on the reality of the day, rather than on preconceived prejudice of what one prefers to believe. Possibly the best guide is to measure any inspiration to action in terms of self-interest. The more people that benefit, the better the action. Surely, the old Hebrew maxim, "Do unto others as you would have them do unto you," is as applicable today as it was 2,500 years ago. Note that sometimes a motivation that appears to be purely individual self-interest may benefit the many.

Example: a person who risks everything he has in order to start a new business is motivated by a passionate desire to have wealth and prestige. The business becomes a huge success and creates many new jobs and opportunities for hundreds or even thousands of other people.

It is certainly easier to find fault with the other man's religion than with one's own beliefs. The Bible has Jesus allude to this in Matthew 7 and Luke 6 by asking why one sees the spec in his neighbor's eye, but not the log in one's own eye.

The simple definition of a Christian is one who follows the teachings of Jesus; Catholics, Mormons and Jehovah Witnesses claim to do this. Yet many of the numerous other so-called Christian denominations would disagree, positing that Mormons are following the teachings of Joseph Smith, Jr. and his successors, while the Jehovah Witnesses follow the Watchtower and Bible Tract Society teachings. Roman Catholics are accused of following the dictates of the Papacy.

The first time I read about the big eternal families that Mormons expect to have in heaven, I thought of a lot of practical problems. For instance, if children are sealed to parents, what about when they grow up, marry and have children of their own? The fathers have been sealed to a different family than their wife, and now their children are to be bonded to them. Or, what about when a Mormon-sealed marriage results in divorce which is allowed by the Mormon church? Which parent do children follow that are sealed to parents of that divorce? It gets more complicated when each parent remarries and has more children while still remaining faithful to Mormonism.

The Mormon church has a process to unseal a marriage, but that does not solve other sticky problems. For example, a faithful Mormon couple are just not compatible and are very unhappy being together. Assume they are killed in a car wreck while still married to each other; are they still sealed to each other for all eternity? How does the Mormon church respond to such questions? About the only answer that I found approximates: "God will have to sort all that out. Humans cannot know everything."

Jehovah Witnesses have regularly been criticized for their many mistaken predictions about the return of Jesus and the end times. In spite of these pretty plain errors in their message, the Jehovah witnesses – like Mormons – have grown considerably in recent years, which may prove that when it comes to religion, error can coexist as truth or together with truth if enough effort is made to proselytize. I read somewhere that Jehovah Witnesses averaged knocking on almost 750 doors for each new member that this effort produces. I suspect that Mormons require a similar effort for each new member. But cannot errors be found in any of the thousands of Christian denominations? While the Catholic half or so of Christianity is not nearly as fragmented as the rest of Christianity, every sect has some erroneous teachings.

The major one may concern the true gospel of Jesus. *The Urantia Book*, to which a later chapter is devoted, best explains it on pages 1670-71:

> Jesus understood the minds of men. He knew what was in the heart of man, and had his teachings been left as he presented them, the only commentary being the inspired interpretation afforded by his earth life, all nations and all religions of the world would speedily have embraced the gospel of the kingdom. The well-meant efforts of Jesus' early followers to restate his teachings so as to make them the more acceptable to certain nations, races, and religions, only resulted in making such teachings the less acceptable to all other nations, races, and religions.

The Apostle Paul, in his efforts to bring the teachings of Jesus to the favorable notice of certain groups in his day, wrote many letters of instruction and admonition. Other teachers of Jesus' gospel did likewise, but none of them realized that some of these writings would subsequently be brought together by those who would set them forth as the embodiment of the teachings of Jesus. And so, while so-called Christianity does contain more of the Master's Gospel than any other religion, it does also contain much that Jesus did not teach. Aside from the incorporation of many teachings from the Persian mysteries and much of the Greek philosophy into early Christianity, two great mistakes were made:

1. The effort to connect the gospel teachings directly onto the Jewish theology, as illustrated by the Christian doctrine of the atonement – the teaching that Jesus was the sacrificed Son who would satisfy the Father's stern justice and appease the divine wrath. These teachings originated in a praiseworthy effort to make the gospel of the kingdom more acceptable to disbelieving Jews. Though these efforts failed as far as winning the Jews were concerned, they did not fail to confuse and alienate many honest souls in all subsequent generations.

2. The second great blunder of the Master's early followers, and one which all subsequent generations have perpetuated, was to organize the Christian teaching so completely about the Person of Jesus. This overemphasis of the personality of Jesus in the theology of Christianity has worked to obscure his teachings, and all of this has made it

increasingly difficult for Jews, Mohammedans, Hindus, and other Eastern religionists to accept the teachings of Jesus. We would not belittle the place of the Person of Jesus in a religion which might bear his name, but we would not permit such consideration to eclipse his inspired life or to supplant his saving message: the fatherhood of God and the brotherhood of man.

The teachers of the religion of Jesus should approach other religions with the recognition of the truths which are held in common (many of which come directly or indirectly from Jesus' message) while they refrain from placing so much emphasis on the differences.

Neither Judaism nor Christianity has revealed an afterlife that offers real intellectual comfort, at least to me, and surely not from the evidence explored in this book thus far. I now turn to other voices.

4 OTHER VOICES

D oes the second largest religion in the world, Islam, with over one and one third billion followers, offer enlightenment about the next life? To the best of my knowledge there is little difference between Muslim and Christian views on the hereafter.

Both Christianity and Islam hold that our final destination is either paradise (heaven) or hell. Of course, there are major differences between the two religions in some of the details of what should be done in this life to gain merit for judgment in the next life. The biggest theological difference is Christianity's rejection of Mohammed and the Koran and Islam's rejection of Jesus' divinity. To the Western mind another of the most objectionable Islamic teachings is that of *jihad*, the holy war against unbelievers – notwithstanding that, in the ancient past, Judaism – and later, Christianity – found *jihad* acceptable. Nor did either religion appear to adhere to Islamic law's mandate concerning a valid *jihad* – that of force being limited to only the necessary amount required to drive off the enemy.

Muslims accept parts of the Bible as holy text, believing they descended from the patriarch Abraham through his first son Ishmael, while Jewish ancestry is traced through his son Isaac. The brothers had different mothers. Muslims refer to God as Allah and some Christian evangelists have gone so far as to call Allah a false god, which in fact would also be calling the Judeo-Christian God false. Why? Because all three religions believe in the monotheistic god of Abraham, regardless of the name He is given. Thus, clerics on either side of this issue would be falsifying their own God by making any designation of Abraham's deity the target of falsification. Naturally, either side might still have some false teachings

49

about that deity. Islam accepts both Jesus and Moses as great prophets, while the Islamic mind sees Mohammed as the last and greatest of the prophets.

The words of the Koran (also spelled Quran) are believed to have been communicated by God's angel Gabriel to Mohammed. But like Jesus with the Bible, Mohammed himself did not pen one word of the Koran. He was said to be illiterate. Christians believe God inspired all the biblical authors, while Muslims see the Koran as containing Allah's exact words to Mohammed, even though written by others and is not in chronological order.

Muslims view the Bible as containing much error. For instance, Genesis 22:2 has God telling Abraham to take his only son Isaac to offer him as a burnt offering. Genesis 22:12 and 16 have the angel of the Lord again specifically refer to Isaac as Abraham's only son. At least, the old *King James* and modern *New Revised Standard* versions of the Bible put it that way. Some modern Bibles, such as the *Catholic New American* or Jewish *Tanakah*, rephrase Genesis 22:2, 12 and 16 to compensate for a problem. Naturally, Muslims take any reference to Isaac being Abraham's only or most loved son as an error and as an insult to their ancestor Ishmael. The Bible plainly tells of Ishmael being Abraham's son whose mother is Hagar, a slave girl of Abraham's wife Sarah, while the Bible story of Hagar and Ishmael is somewhat convoluted, it being mentioned in several chapters of Genesis. There is no question that Ishmael was Abraham's first son. Christian scholars justify the literal error of "only son" with meanings such as "only son of the promise," "uniquely precious" and "especially loved." Our old friend Dr. Halley in his *Handbook* sees the offering of Isaac as "a picture-prophecy of the death of Christ." Halley ignored any commentary about the problem of Isaac being the only son. Muslim thought may see Ishmael, not Isaac, as the son chosen by God to test Abraham.

Consider the division between the world's two largest religions concerning *jihad*. There is no question that

Mohammed was a warrior and a very good one as evidenced by his military achievements. Certainly his teachings about God would incorporate his militaristic experience as well as his experience as a ruler.

Most everyone has heard that Muslim martyrs are rewarded in heaven with seventy-two virgins, at least, this applied to male martyrs. Some say that this is a mistranslation. Presently, in any case, details of the heavenly reward are not as important as the earthly action it takes to get to heaven.

The teaching of *jihad* and how it is understood in this day is not consistent within Islam. Some moderate Muslims hold that Islam is a religion of peace and *jihad* should be invoked only as a defensive measure. *Jihad* means to struggle or strive for right change – God's way. This struggle can mean exerting one's self to live the way God wills – to follow the teachings and example of Mohammed. In particular, in defense of Islam, it is generally called holy war. Notwithstanding that this traditionally addressed defensive action only; violent offensive action has at times during history and currently been used by those twisting Islamic teaching to fit a particular agenda, such as that of Osama bin Laden. Those who prefer to see Islam as a religion of war and terror usually point to the so-called sword verses, Koranic chapter 9 verse 5, which in part says to slay the unbelievers wherever you find them. And a partial rendering of verse 9:29 instructs to fight those who do not believe in Allah nor in the last day. Utilizing a common tendency to quote holy texts to suit one's needs, both verses contain moderation that is usually ignored. What follows in verse 9:5? If they repent . . . then open the way for them: for God is often forgiving, most merciful. Verse 9:29 also admonishes fighting until they pay the *jizya* (poll tax) with willing submission, and feel themselves subdued. To better understand the opposing interpretations that have been derived concerning these verses, one has only to look on the internet.

The Koran, like both Testaments in the Bible, contains verses that can be quoted to justify slaughtering unbelievers if that is one's preferred purpose. I already discussed God ordering Moses and Joshua to slaughter non-Jews and also Jews who strayed from God's path with a golden idol as portrayed in the Old Testament. In the New Testament, consider: Luke 19:27 which ends a parable with Jesus saying to bring His enemies who did not want Him as their King and slaughter them in his presence. Matthew 10:34 has Jesus telling His disciples not to think He has come to bring peace, but a sword. Note that today no significant Jewish or Christian group attempts to justify terrorism or murder by quoting Holy Scripture. Some might endorse the death penalty with scripture, but that is a different matter. Terrorists may justify their horrific acts by seeing themselves as defending Islamic land from the imperialistic invaders from the United States and its allies. Of course, suicide bombers ignore or are ignorant of the fact that the Muslim consequence of suicide in any form is eternal damnation. From Princeton professor Bernard Lewis' book, *The Crisis of Islam*, we are told that Islam considers suicide to be a mortal sin and earns eternal damnation even for those who would otherwise have gone to paradise.

Additionally, we are informed that the classical Islamic jurists clearly made the distinction between facing certain death from the enemy's hand and death from committing suicide. One's eternal future of heaven or hell was at stake. Also, that some recent fundamentalist Islamic jurists and others have blurred or even dismissed this distinction. Lewis' book points out that Islamic law enjoins warriors in a *jihad* not to kill women, children and the aged unless they attack first. His text reads: "At no point do the basic texts of Islam enjoin terrorism and murder." The Wall Street Journal calls professor Lewis, "the world's foremost Islamic scholar." His short book is most informative on a subject that most of us need more knowledge about and a subject that the G. W. Bush administration should have better understood before invading Iraq. Interestingly, professor Lewis became an important advisor to President Bush.

Why are Muslims who teach peace not highly vocal about the ultimate fate of *jihadists* who commit suicide winding up in hell? Professor Lewis strongly points out that Islamic teachings do not support heavenly rewards for suicide martyrs – just the opposite. Consider, is the suicide bomber so indoctrinated that his mind is void of counter-logic? Such as, when he supposedly wakes up in paradise does he have any concern about possibly encountering some of his innocent victims of which many are also Muslims? The fact is terrorists have been indoctrinated by their superiors to believe that other Muslims or anyone else who disagrees with the terrorists' version of *jihad* are heretics and enemies of God. Therefore, *jihad* against these sinners is justified, and, of course, enemies of God do not go to heaven. Some Muslims, like those of other faiths, put their own twist of interpretation on authoritative texts. The justification for their own agenda may be in direct opposition to what the author of the text actually meant.

The Christian and Islamic paths to heaven are very different. The Christian way is only through acceptance of Jesus as the Savior who washed away our sins through His tragic death as interpreted from the Bible. The Muslim way is following divine instructions believed to have been given Mohammed as presented in the Koran, which clearly includes *jihad*. In this day Christianity has no concept comparable to that of *jihad*. When combined, the Christian and Islamic religions encompass over one half of the world's population that is currently estimated at 6.6 billion. Both teach that our eternal future is either a joyous heaven or a horrific hell.

What about the third and fourth largest religions, that is, Hinduism and Buddhism? Hindus outnumber Buddhists over two to one. Together they account for almost one fifth of the world's population. Generally, neither of the two agrees with the Christian and Islamic views of an afterlife. Nor do either have a single holy book that is the source of fixed dogma; rather, both have numerous texts that are accepted as authoritative guides. At least one school, that of zen Buddhism, dismisses all sacred writings as a valid path to enlightenment. Siddharth Gautama, who founded Buddhism over 2,500 years ago, did so as a protest against Hinduism – the world's oldest known religion. His teachings were practical instructions that avoided Hinduism's complexity of teachings, rituals and practices. Gautama's purpose was to escape selfish desire that he saw as the source of all suffering.

Over time, much Buddhist thought has incorporated a great deal of Hindu complexity as well as being influenced by other religious thought. Thus, today like all the major religions, Buddhism and Hinduism each have various schools of thought and differences. Gautama became known as the Buddha, which means the enlightened one or the awakened one. Obviously, this is the source of Buddhism's name. Since Buddha's original teachings did not include a supernatural god of any sort, some call Buddhism a philosophy rather than a religion. However, today some elements of Buddhism do include a divine being or even a host of gods. The more enlightened teachers of eastern religion generally see multiple gods as different aspects of one single god. Interestingly, Buddhism does not posit a single god as creator of the universe. In any case, I find it difficult to separate any religion from philosophy. The best definition for theology that I know of comes from *The Urantia Book*, that is, the philosophy of religion.

While these two eastern religions, Hinduism and Buddhism, have much similarity, considerable differences can be found within the various sects. Generally, these two eastern religions agree on the final goal of the afterlife – liberation from the cycle of reincarnating. Both Hinduism and Buddhism have reincarnation as a core concept. After physical death, Hinduism teaches that the atman (soul) takes on a new physical existence. This existence is usually another human. But according to this way of thinking it is possible to come back as an animal, insect, plant or even an inanimate object. It all depends on one's *karma*, the alleged force that has been shaped by the sum total of the soul's previous action and experience.

The Buddha's reincarnation teaching was quite different. He taught that there is no eternal soul; rather, in its place there is an ongoing series of connected lives. When a person dies, Buddhism teaches that that moment in time creates the birth of another person. While there is no permanent, unchanging soul that takes on a new personality with each death and rebirth, there is a continuing sequence at death of the old personality producing a new one. Some have described it as the flame of a dying candle being used to light a new candle.

Buddhism does not deny the Hindu concept of reincarnation, but gives its own twist of complexity to the possibility. The Tibetan Dalai Lama and his predecessors are generally seen as the continuing rebirth of the same being. As well, the Buddhist text *The Tibetan Book of the Dead* describes the immediate afterlife experience in terms of a continuing being in transition. A deceased person that has been insufficiently trained in spiritual practices can encounter some temporary or even permanent horror, such as, hungry ghosts as named by *The Book of the Dead*. A properly trained living person can give the dead person instructions on how to obtain salvation or liberation during the transition period. These instructions must begin immediately after death or while dying. Like Hinduism's concept of the living world being an illusion, Buddhism sees any horror in the afterlife as illusionary, although the deceased person that is experiencing such nightmares, suffers them as a reality. Also, there is a body of texts about Buddha's previous lives. Such elements blur the difference between Hinduism's permanent soul and Buddhism's connected lives.

In Buddhism and Hinduism it is thought that only through dedication to various practices such as meditation and yoga can one gain the spiritual insight to escape the ongoing cycle of continuation of death and new birth. According to Buddhism, the ultimate place or state where all suffering, individual passion and delusion ends, is called *nirvana*. Hinduism calls it *moksha*, also spelled *moksa*.

We should note that neither Jesus, nor Buddha, or Mohammed left any written records of their own. All their doings and teachings were written down by others, much of which was passed verbally many times before it was reduced to writing. The same could be said about Moses, as most independent scholars, as well as others, agree he did not write the first five books of the Old Testament – notwithstanding that orthodox Christianity and orthodox Judaism would disagree. Additionally, consider that the Koran was committed to writing during Mohammed's lifetime, even though there was said to be several versions. Hinduism cannot be traced to any single founder or dominant personality.

There is some similarity with *nirvana-moksha* and the Christian-Islamic view of heaven, that is, total freedom from pain, sorrow and worry for all who obtain the afterlife's greatest reward. Of course, even the atheistic view that death annihilates all possible experience for the dead person, would produce the same freedom from pain, sorrow and worry.

Does the atheist have anything to tell us about the next life? Only that he believes there is not one. Many atheists accept the philosophy of Karl Marx in that religion is the opium of the masses, in other words, it gives comfort to believe that death is not the termination of existence. The continuation of the soul, personality, atman, or whatever it's called, is thought by some to be man's motivation for creating religion. Many atheists think that religion is actually good and necessary for most folks, but they themselves can find their comfort in science and reality. Interestingly, surveys have shown that atheists equal the religious in some areas of morality. Somewhere I saw a creditable survey that showed fundamentalist and mainline Christians with a higher divorce rate than that of atheists.

Motivated by religionists' attacks on science, as well as a common ignorance of science, and by the claimed miracle cures of the sick through television evangelists, and other perceived deception generated by religion, some prominent atheists have become highly vocal in striking back. Perhaps the most known atheist and one of the most knowledgeable is Richard Dawkins. He was the Charles Simonyi professor of the public understanding of science at Oxford University. His best seller book *The God Delusion* gives a wealth of information on the scientific response to many matters related to religion. His book gives abundant evidence in support of his position. Most atheists would agree with professor Dawkins when he says, on page 190, "the idea of immortality itself survives and spreads because it caters to wishful thinking." Yet some atheists disagree with the strength of his attack on religion. But from what I know, the professor's dialogue is no stronger than some religionists' rhetoric against him or against science. I believe that anyone on either side of the religious issue may gain a useful understanding of science and why professor Dawkins chose atheism by simply reading *The God Delusion*.

The handicap that most heavily indoctrinated religionists have is that of a fixed truth built around a lack of compromise. One manifestation of this is that of picking passages from texts that best support their truth and ignoring passages and other evidence that tend to question it. Surprisingly, I saw a similar example of this technique used by professor Dawkins on page 12 of *The God Delusion*. He quotes the closing lines of *The Origin of Species* – Charles Darwin's famous book. One part Dawkins has as "having been originally breathed into a few forms or into one."

My copy of *The Origin of Species* reads, "having been originally breathed by the Creator into a few forms or into one." My copy is the sixth edition of *The Origin of Species*. Dawkins' quote is from the first edition that was published in November 1859 and consisted of 1,250 copies. Due to its sales success, a second edition of 3,000 copies was published less than two months later. In this edition, the words "by the Creator" were added into the closing sentence. The first five editions carried the full title: *On The Origin of Species by Means of Natural Selection, or The Preservation of Favored Races in the Struggle For Life.* In 1872 with the publication of the sixth edition the title was changed to *The Origin of Species.* Dawkins, as well as others, have interpreted this "Creator " addition as an indication that Darwin gave in to religious pressure. However, that does not appear to be the case since the first edition refers to the term "Creator" on several occasions. My thinking is that Dawkins prefers the original quote while using the latter title simply because his belief is fixed against a Creator.

At this juncture I will review my exploration of eternity. Heaven or hell is the dominant view of most folks, at least, that is what their religions teach. Hinduism's 880 million or so adherents and Buddhism's 400 million commonly see *nirvana-moksha* as the ultimate reward for eternity. The cycle of reincarnation is seen as the negative to the reward of *nirvana-moksha.* It is possible for the most spiritually enlightened to obtain *nirvana-moksha* in this life before physical death. Simply said, Hinduism sees the final stage of enlightenment as the individual soul's merger with the oversoul of all creation. Buddha's original teaching saw ultimate salvation as the cessation of all awareness. To my understanding, this is the same as the prevailing atheistic view of today, the difference being that Buddha saw a sequence of related lives leading up to nirvana. In contrast, the atheist believes in only one time around for the individual, but some understand that one's DNA sequences into the future with the production of offspring.

Generally, Hinduism's teaching is fuzzy about distinguishing between annihilation of individual experience and the continued experience by the merged soul. As is the case, with so much else in Hinduism, one is offered a choice about what to believe concerning conscious awareness during eternal life. In the ninth century CE, Shankara formulated the Advaita (non-dual) which says that our soul and God are one and the same in substance. Some three centuries later the great sage Ramanuja formulated the teachings of Vistishtadvaita, which make a distinction in the Advaita's teaching of non-duality by holding that the soul maintains its individual self-consciousness while at the same time being in an eternal relationship with God Who is the same substance as the soul.

Some teach it is like the merger of a raindrop with the ocean. The raindrop still exists, but as part of the ocean. Of course, as far as we know a raindrop never has any awareness of experience and this example would say nothing about human intelligence and possible afterlife awareness. Even though the twists and turns on the path to enlightenment and permanence in the afterlife vary within and between Buddhism and Hinduism, their common view on *nirvana-moksha* is one of ultimate bliss – liberation – salvation. All passion, pain, suffering and worry cease once *nirvana-moksha* is obtained.

The atheist says that total cessation of any possible future awareness accompanies the death of any individual. There is no question that this view would also end all passion, pain, suffering and worry – at least, for the dead person. However, is that the same as ultimate bliss or liberation? In my mind, bliss or liberation must be experienced in some form of intelligent awareness. The same could be said of passion, pain, suffering and worry. But the difference is that these emotions or feelings terminate in *nirvana-moksha*, while bliss or liberation begin. This might be a play on words, but perhaps it demonstrates a real difference between the atheistic view of eternity and that of Hinduism as well as some Buddhist thought.

Assuming that eternal bliss can be experienced in conscious awareness, akin to human intelligence, what purpose would it serve? What purpose does the Christian-Islamic view of heaven satisfy? In both cases, it seems the answer is as a reward for taking the right spiritual path. By extension of this thinking, perhaps the purpose of life is to seek reward. Some would counter why does life need a purpose? Purpose supporters at some point must include a Supreme Being or force that drives all purpose. The opposition can settle for there is no purpose to life – it just is. Judeo-Christian-Islamic thinking invokes the God of Abraham as the driver of all purpose. Christianity personalized God in the divine person of Jesus of Nazareth, whereas Judaism's mighty hero, Moses, is only God's messenger. Islam also sees its greatest prophet, Mohammed, as God's messenger. Judaism does not focus on a heaven or hell theology, while heaven or hell is central to Christian and Islamic teachings.

Buddhism-Hinduism's driving force is viewed as the ultimate force of all creation and it manifests as *karma* within the physical world, at least within the understanding of some humans that see it as a single force that drives all creation. Hindus tend to personalize this one force into three main aspects or deities. Brahma – the creator; Vishnu – the maintainer or preserver; and Shiva is seen as the destroyer or transformer. The personal is taken one step further in stories of Krishna who is seen as the incarnation, in human form, of the god Vishnu. Hindu belief has the flexibility to accommodate almost any individual understanding of the one great force. Hindu tradition allows for 330 million gods. This incredible number of gods and their respective images is the main cause of misunderstanding by other religious believers. They take Hinduism to be a primitive belief of millions of gods and idols. The understanding Hindu sees them as different forms of the one great force – ultimate reality. No amount of thought or number of gods can ever overcome the mystery surrounding the one great force Hinduism calls Brahman.

Life's purpose appears to terminate when one advances to the highest level of spiritual enlightenment and merges for all eternity with that one force. Interestingly, when all is said and done, purpose or no purpose ultimately ends at the same point – either nature is or God is. Any attempt to go beyond this point results in infinite regress. In other words, if God created nature, then who-what created God? Then, the question continually repeats in asking who-what created the last who-what. If you reverse the puzzle to ask if nature was the ultimate force that created God, you get the same endless result.

I have now explored some belief of over seventy percent of the world's population as commonly taught by the four largest religions. The roughly fourteen to sixteen million Jews in the world today represent less than one fourth of one percent of the world's population, the majority of whom cling to Judaism more as a heritage and social function rather than a strong religious guide. In any case, Judaism has had a vast influence on shaping the teachings of Christianity and Islam, and they in turn have affected today's Judaism. Atheists possibly represent three to four percent of our planet's people. Others who claim no religious affiliation represent perhaps another twelve percent. Numerous other religions or philosophies instruct the remaining people of our planet.

The next chapter explores a little known source that contains a whole lot of information. It is so important and unusual that it is said to be supernatural revelation to our planet.

5 THE URANTIA BOOK

The Urantia Book consists of 2,097 pages. It was compiled from 196 papers credited to 23 authors. But not authors in the normal sense – all *The Urantia Book* authors are said to be supernatural beings. They are known as: Divine Counselor, Universal Censor, Perfector of Wisdom, Mighty Messenger, One High in Authority, One Without Name and Number, Chief of Archangels, Vorondadek Son, Brilliant Evening Star, Melchizedek, Archangel, Malavatia Melchizedek, Secondary Lanonandek, Manovandet Melchizedek, Machiventa Melchizedek, Life Carrier, Solonia, Chief of Seraphim, Chief of Midwayers, Solitary Messenger, Chief of Evening Stars, Mantutia Melchizedek, and the Midwayer Commission. Most of these names refer to a group of beings and different individuals of the same order may be referred to by the same name, the exceptions being the four Melchizedeks that have first names, Solonia that is from the seraphim group and any chief of a group.

The book contains the Foreword and four main parts: Part I, The Central and Super Universes; Part II, The Local Universe; Part III, The History of Urantia; and Part IV, The Life and Teachings of Jesus. A flavor of *The Urantia Book* is conveyed by the first page of the Foreword:

> In the minds of the mortals of Urantia – that being the name of your world – there exists great confusion respecting the meaning of such terms as God, divinity and deity. Human beings are still more confused and uncertain about the relationships of the divine personalities designated by these numerous appellations. Because of this conceptual poverty

associated with so much ideational confusion, I have been directed to formulate this introductory statement in explanation of the meanings which should be attached to certain word symbols as they may be hereinafter used in these papers which the Orvonton corps of truth revealers have been authorized to translate into the English language of *Urantia*.

It is exceedingly difficult to present enlarged concepts and advanced truth in our endeavor to expand cosmic consciousness and enhance spiritual perception, when we are restricted to the use of a circumscribed language of the realm. But our mandate admonishes us to make every effort to convey our meanings by using the word symbols of the English tongue. We have been instructed to introduce new terms only when the concept to be portrayed finds no terminology in English which can be employed to convey such a new concept partially or even with more or less distortion of meaning.

In the hope of facilitating comprehension and of preventing confusion on the part of every mortal who may peruse these papers, we deem it wise to present in this initial statement an outline of the meanings to be attached to numerous English words which are to be employed in designation of Deity and certain associated concepts of the things, meanings, and values of universal reality.

But in order to formulate this Foreword of definitions and limitations of terminology, it is necessary to anticipate the usage of these terms in the subsequent presentations. This Foreword is not, therefore, a finished statement within itself; it is only a definitive guide designed to assist those who shall read the accompanying papers dealing with Deity and the universe of universes which have been formulated by an Orvonton commission sent to Urantia for this purpose.

Your world, Urantia, is one of many similar inhabited planets which comprise the local universe of Nebadon. This universe, together with similar creations, make up the superuniverse of Orvonton from whose capital, Uversa, our commission hails. Orvonton is one of the seven evolutionary superuniverses of time and space which circle the never-beginning, never-ending creation of divine perfection – the central universe of Havona. At the heart of this eternal and central universe is the stationary Isle of Paradise, the geographic center of infinity and the dwelling place of the eternal God.

The seven evolving superuniverses in association with the central and divine universe, we commonly refer to as the grand universe; these are the now organized and inhabited creations. They are all a part of the master universe, which also embraces the uninhabited but mobilizing universes of outer space.

This first page of the Foreword is easier to understand than most of its remaining sixteen pages. Yet, it gives the impression that any reader of *The Urantia Book* is in for a difficult read. It is true that many of its disclosures are very hard to understand, while much of its information is easily grasped.

As the authors are said to be supernatural, how was their information passed and published? The story goes that it was transmitted in conjunction with a human subject while in a sleep state. This human was to remain unnamed so as to avoid any person being venerated in regards to *The Urantia Book*. It is said the information appeared in various ways. For many years unusual information came from the sleeping subject that developed into a question-and-answer type of communication. Then, around 1925, the first written paper appeared. The details on the written paper's appearances are unknown. But on one occasion, it is said almost 500 pages appeared overnight. On another occasion, papers supposedly appeared in a locked safe. Everyone who participated in acquiring the Urantia papers claimed not to know the technique involved.

It all began in the early 1900s when William S. Sadler, MD discovered that one of his patients revealed unusual information while sleeping. Sadler's religious background was that of a Seven Day Adventist. He was, however, somewhat skeptical of that religion's acceptance of Ellen White as a prophetess who received divinely transmitted revelations. Sadler actively investigated and debunked the paranormal, particularly that of channeling through a medium. He was said to be truly puzzled by the unique revelations coming from his sleeping patient. Throughout Sadlers' long association with the Urantia papers and the book, he maintained that the phenomena associated with his unusual patient was in no way similar to any other well-known type of psychically-received information. It was not automatic writing, clairvoyance, hypnosis, multiple personality, spirit medium-ship, telepathy, nor trances. Sadler stressed that the Urantia papers were not in any way associated with spiritualism, consisting of séances and supposed communication with spirits of the dead.

Sadler became the driving force that resulted in the publication of *The Urantia Book* in 1955. The Urantia foundation was set up as a legal entity in January 1950 to publish and control the rights to the book. It was copyrighted by the foundation in 1955. Part of the foundation's mission was to keep the book inviolate – to keep it undisturbed from the original. In later years, conflict between the foundation and others who wanted to break the foundation's control of the book resulted in court battles and around 2003 the Urantia foundation lost its bid for copyright renewal, at least to the English version of the book in the United States. Since the book has been published in several languages, other copyrights are still in effect.

Back to the Forward, I shall now condense what page one says. In the cosmic scheme, our planet is called Urantia:

it is part of the local universe of Nebadon, which in turn, is part of the superuniverse called Orvonton; it says that a group of truth revealers from Uversa, Orvonton's capital, were authorized to translate into English the papers that became The Urantia Book. Due to being restricted to the English language, and not presenting new terms unless no English term conveyed an appropriate meaning, the truth revealers had a difficult task and therefore felt the need to explain the meanings which should be attached to certain English words as used in their papers. The page also reveals that many inhabited planets besides Earth comprise the local universe of Nebadon. Further, many similar local universes make up a superuniverse, and that seven evolutionary superuniverses of time and space circle the central universe of Havona, at whose heart stands the stationary Isle of Paradise that is the dwelling place of the eternal God. The seven superuniverses, with the central and divine universe, is commonly referred to as the grand universe.

The book itself has much to say about the grand universe, the presently-organized creation which is only a part of the master universe that also includes the uninhabited, but mobilizing universes of outer space. The book advises that the superuniverses are unfinished, new nebulae are still in process. A finished superuniverse will consist of about 100,000 local universes that each will include some 10 million inhabited worlds. That equates to one trillion inhabited worlds in one finished superuniverse. Our superuniverse of Orvonton is said to contain ten trillion suns and have a diameter of roughly 500,000 light years.

For what it is worth, I personally believe Edgar Cayce was the sleeping personality associated with *The Urantia Book*. Cayce did his famous health and life readings while in a self-induced sleeping state during the same period that the Urantia papers appeared. The papers were said to be completed about ten years before Cayce's death in 1945, although editing and other work preparing the papers for publication continued into the 1940s. John M. Bunker and Karen L. Pressler authored the book *Edgar Cayce and The Urantia Book*, which makes a good case that Cayce was the sleeping source. Although science writer and skeptic Martin Gardner, in his book *Urantia*, which is subtitled the *Great Cult Mystery*, names Wilfred Kellogg – Dr. William Sadler's brother-in-law – as the sleeping personality. Sadler's wife Lena was also a medical doctor.

In any case, numerous books have been written and internet information is available concerning *The Urantia Book*. Since my main purpose here is to explore its disclosures regarding the hereafter, I will turn to that subject.

First, it is necessary to understand *The Urantia Book's* disclosure regarding the Thought Adjustor, also known as a Mystery Monitor that is explained as a fragment of God, a divine spirit, that indwells the mind of humans. The book makes clear that God is spirit: "He is a universal, spiritual presence. Spirit beings are real, notwithstanding they are invisible to human eyes; even though they have not flesh and blood." God's fragmentized spirit maintains immediate contact with his creature-children and his created universes.

A Thought Adjustor is said to indwell a normal human mind around the age of five. The purpose is to subtly influence that human's thoughts in the direction of doing God's will. When the human dies the Adjustor returns to God to await possible return and eventual eternal fusion with that human. It all depends on the human's free will choice to do God's will. When a person dies, one's body remains on the earth to return to dust, while the unconscious soul is transported to one of seven so-called mansion worlds. There, the personality is reassembled with a new body that *The Urantia Book* calls *morontia*. This new form is more spiritual and less physical than one's earth body.

The purpose of intelligent life, from the beginning and throughout eternity, is to do God's will. Intelligent will creatures, such as human beings on earth, start out their career on one of the trillions of worlds in a universe of universes. The duty of all will creatures is found in the New Testament instruction of Matthew 5:48, that is, to be perfect as the Heavenly Father is perfect.

The Urantia Book details a cosmic government structure that starts at the planetary level and ascends a celestial order all the way to paradise. Each one of the seven superuniverses contains the following levels and names the ruling body:

planet	planetary prince
system	system sovereign
constellation	constellation fathers
local universe	creator son
minor sector	recents of days
major sector	perfections of days
superuniverse	ancients of days

The creature with a will, who has experienced physical death on a planet and whose soul survives, begins the long career of ascending his particular superuniverse. From the time the soul awakens in a *morontia* body on the first mansion world, which is located in a local system, its purpose is to grow in knowledge and progress from world to world while advancing to higher levels in the superuniverse. Early in this journey the original Thought Adjustor rejoins this new ascending *morontia* being. And once that being unconditionally decides to survive by doing God's will, the Thought Adjustor and that being are merged as one for all eternity. As the creature's knowledge increases in understanding God's will that same creature becomes more spiritual and less physical until ultimately becoming pure spirit being that is actually capable of seeing God. Eternal life as a pure spirit is spent with specific responsibilities in service to God's divine plan. Once the ascending being has completed a superuniverse education, the next stop is Havona, which is located in the central universe. Here, the occupants are said to be so advanced that there is no ruling body; all residents govern themselves. The final destination is the absolute level of paradise, but not the end of the journey. One's eternal service might be required anywhere in the master universe.

The opposing experience to this survival journey is complete annihilation. The annihilated soul simply ceases to be, as if it never existed. However, the cosmos, with all its myriad creations and creatures, is geared or oriented toward the survival of will creatures. In our short existence on earth, the making of an erroneous choice in or about religion will not disqualify the soul's survival. The much more important issue is the desire to know truth. Perhaps humans really begin a religious journey with the recognition of just how partial their truth really is.

In any case, *The Urantia Book* portrays God as the universal Father who loves every single one of his creature-children and who has staffed the entire cosmos with a vast number and kind of material and spiritual beings. They interface in varying ways with divinity. This same God provides impersonal energy to power all that is and all that will be. Humans need only to exercise their free will to accept the Father's free gift of survival. This is accomplished by continually choosing to do God's will. Perhaps we only gain a small glimpse of what that really means during our current life.

The Urantia Book gives the most detailed history of creation and cosmology mixed with religion and the afterlife that I have ever found. The book does state that its cosmology is not inspired, which appears to mean, not divinely inspired. Thus, new scientific discoveries will require cosmological updates. At the same time, the book states that the historical facts and religious truths of its revelation will stand on the records of the ages to come.

Since much of its story includes previously unknown beings and events, we have no frame of reference to prove or disprove their reality. So why should we believe anything disclosed in *The Urantia Book*? The same question applied to the Bible gives us a basis for an answer. Outside of the Bible, there is no supporting evidence that the majority of holy people mentioned ever existed. Nor is there scientific proof that even one of the so-called miracles as related in the Bible ever actually occurred. Thus, *The Urantia Book* and the Bible itself must be subject to individual belief. I am confident that if the Bible had never been composed and instead, nineteen hundred years ago, *The Urantia Book*, adjusted to that time in history, came to be, more of the world's population would accept *The Urantia Book* as holy text than adhere to the Bible today. In fact, *The Urantia Book* gives a much clearer, detailed story of Jesus' life, death and purpose. In *The Urantia Book's* version, as a Creator Son, He is ranked very high in the divine order. But He is not said to be God Himself or a part of the Trinity, while at the same time He is recognized as having earned sovereignty of our local universe through the divine plan of guiding its creation and the personal experience, over eons of time, of incarnating as an actual being of several orders of universe inhabitants. His final incarnation was as a human in the Person of Jesus of Nazareth. Thus, He is portrayed in *The Urantia Book* as Lord of our local universe, but subservient to God the Father – the First Cause – Who is the supreme Lord of the master universe. *The Urantia Book* claims there are several hundred thousand creator sons, of the same order as Jesus, at work in the cosmos. As to Old Testament times, its characters and events are portrayed by *The Urantia Book* in more realistic terms with much less repetition than the Bible. Like the Bible, *The Urantia Book* includes supernatural action. I shall close this chapter with a paragraph from page 26 of *The Urantia Book*:

> When you are through down here, when your course has been run in temporary form on earth, when your trial trip in the flesh is finished, when the dust that composes the mortal tabernacle "returns to the earth whence it came"; then, it is revealed, the indwelling

"Spirit shall return to God who gave it." There sojourns within each mortal being of this planet a fragment of God, a part and parcel of divinity. It is not yet yours by right of possession, but it is designedly intended to be one with you if you survive the mortal existence.

6 CONSCIOUSNESS OR FORCE

P reviously, I said that any answers to the hereafter are only human speculation. There is presently no way to verify anything about the next life – if there is one. The best one can do is *guess*, even if the most knowledgeable experts' opinions or accepted sacred text are the basis of one's guessing.

I will change course for a while and explore the here and now.

There are over six and a half billion human beings presently inhabiting our world. Every one of them came into being by the same means, that is, a male sperm fertilized a woman's egg. A new physical body then developed within the fertilized female's body. Some months later, a new human came forth from his mother's womb. The sex act was responsible for most babies. In some cases, medical science introduced the sperm into the egg. There is the possibility that a person may have or soon may come into being by cloning.

No one knows exactly when the developing fetus becomes conscious or able to experience. Perhaps it is not until birth when all life support from the mother is terminated. Yes, there is medical equipment that shows heartbeat, brain wave activity and other functions that many accept as the developing fetus being alive. But no one can say with certainty that the unborn child ever has any conscious experience. Whenever experience or awareness first functions in a new being, the big question is, where did it come from? Did the newly-developed brain produce the consciousness or mind? Some argue that it is the other way around: the consciousness created the brain or at least utilizes the brain as a physical receiver that transmits information to the physical body.

The science of neurology says that the physical brain generates the mind. According to Gary E. Schwartz, Ph.D., in his book with William L. Simon, entitled *The G.O.D. Experiments*, he says on page 208 that no one has explained the origin of human consciousness in physical terms. The subtitle of his book is *How Science Is Discovering God in Everything Including Us*.

This seems to indicate that Schwartz is trying to prove God scientifically, however, that is not the case. On page 158 he states that he is not trying to use science to prove God's existence. Instead, he claims to open-mindedly be using scientific method to let God – if He exists – prove His own existence. I submit that there is a much easier and more effective way for God to do that, which I'll get to later.

Dr. Schwartz is a good example of a well-trained and experienced scientist that has not closed his mind to God. But his book is not about the Biblical God. G.O.D. represents a *Guiding-Organizing-Designing* process as a specific concept. Dr. Schwartz is dedicated to scientific principles. Now, other scientists can confirm or refute his evidence. He makes a case that order does not occur by chance, rather that chance produces the opportunity for creative orders to happen which are governed by a Guiding-Organizing-Designing, universal field process.

Where mainstream science and Schwartz disagree, in my understanding, is not that chance produces order, but that science says that the process of natural selection is the producer of order while Schwartz suggests an intelligent, organizing universal field as the cause.

Richard Dawkins' *The God Delusion* has a subchapter on page 119 entitled *Irreducible Complexity* that articulately addresses chance, natural selection and intelligent design.

Is a universal G.O.D. process that guides, organizes and designs all creation as envisioned by Schwartz really any different than Hinduism's oversoul of all creation or the force behind Buddhism's sequence of connected lives? Or the Lord-God of Judeo-Christian-Islamic thinking – especially the view held by many Christians of how the Holy Spirit interfaces with them to guide, organize and design their lives? The main distinction in these views appears to concern if that ultimate, controlling force is personal or impersonal. Is it conscious?

A person is generally defined as a human being, as opposed to an animal. When the concept of personal is used as descriptive of the ultimate force in the universe, I mean to convey a consciousness that thinks, reasons and acts in a manner that is understood in human terms as intelligent. Impersonal, in this sense, would mean a force that is pure energy and always functions in the same unchanging way with no regard to reason, logic, feelings or emotions.

Hinduism's ultimate force – Brahman – is seen as impersonal. But as already mentioned, Hindus generally give personality to this one force in the form of three main Gods, while allowing for 330 million aspects of these three gods. The god Vishnu, similar to Christian teachings about Jesus, sometimes incarnates as a human. A paradox is presented when the individual soul is liberated in the final stage of enlightenment because one's personal soul is then merged with the impersonal Brahman. Shankara's teaching of non-duality would require the annihilation of a merged soul's personality, while Ramanuja's view that the soul maintains its self-consciousness during its eternal relationship as a part of the Brahman seems to nullify the one great force as remaining impersonal – particularly, since each incoming soul would include personality.

Why does it matter if creation's strongest force is impersonal or personal? For the same reason it is relevant to know if the brain produces the mind or the mind uses the brain as a receiver and transmitter. If a physical brain created and maintains our mind, our consciousness, then when that brain dies and stops all functions, so does the mind. If the eternal force of all creation is impersonal then there is no survival of personality which appears to eliminate all possible consciousness for any dead being. Interestingly, Buddha's original concept of final enlightenment being the cessation of all awareness, would be in harmony with the view of an eternal, impersonal Brahman. So it seems that God, or the eternal, absolute principle in the universe, has to be personal if there is to be any afterlife survival of human consciousness in any form.

Professor Schwartz is plainly proposing a G.O.D. process that is intelligent. The epilog to his book is titled *Infinite Love: The Ultimate Gift From G.O.D.?* An impersonal force cannot love, nor can it hate. Judeo-Christian-Islamic traditions have always conveyed concepts of a personal God. Many times, He is portrayed as all-too personal in taking on all the characteristics of man. Islam objects to any form being attached to God. In Islamic thought, God is considered to be formless and beyond human ability to describe.

The eternal survival of human consciousness is thus dependent on at least one condition: that the mind must exist independent of the physical brain or body. A second condition seems to be that the eternal, absolute principle of the universe must be personal.

What about individual consciousness surviving physical death for a finite period? Reason appears to require that any mind operate without any need for a brain, if consciousness is to survive the brain's death for any period of time. Even so, a receiver-brain appears necessary to transmit consciousness to a material being. Interestingly, Catholicism and other Christians believe in the resurrection of the dead with a restored physical body. This would include the brain. If true, the mind could resume functioning regardless of where consciousness originates. According to *The Urantia Book*, during Jesus' time, the Jewish religious party, the Pharisees, believed in the resurrection of the literal, human body. While the Sadducees, another Jewish group, opposed this view.

An impersonal ultimate force of the universe presents the question: can a blind force be superior to intelligence? Present day science says yes, since science does not require an

Intelligent Designer. Extremely well documented evolution theory explains how all living things have evolved from lesser things in a trial-and-error process of natural selection. This process started with the beginning of time about 14 billion years ago, commonly called the Big Bang. All physical laws are said to break down beyond the instant of this amazing event. Prior to the Big Bang, all the mass or energy in the universe today is said to have been compressed into a space smaller than an atom. This brought some scientists to theorize that a square inch of what is commonly called empty space – or the vacuum of space – actually contains more energy than the entire universe presently utilizes. If this is correct, an impersonal ultimate force could be powerful beyond imagination.

But would this unimaginably powerful energy be superior to an intelligence that can reason, think, change its way or love and hate? My Webster's dictionary defines superior as higher in station, rank, degree, etc."

Based on this meaning, the scientific view of creation having no need of an Intelligent Designer would say that this impersonal force must be superior as it caused the momentum that ultimately resulted in the appearance of intelligence. Or is this the prime example of evolution producing a superior product from a lesser one?

Of course, there are gaps in scientific understanding. For example, what caused the chance occurrence of the Big Bang? If every square inch of space really has the potential to be an even bigger bang, what keeps the incredible number of possibilities from happening?

Theoretical physicists are hard at work on a theory that may explain the Big Bang. It is known as M-theory and it concerns infinitely small, vibrating strings that produce all forms of matter or energy. The "M" of M-theory generally stands for membrane because the theory says that colliding membranes – that were made from these vibrating strings that touch each other – caused the Big Bang. And since these membranes may operate in ten or eleven, or even possibly 26 or more dimensions, Big Bangs could or did happen in other dimensions that our three dimensional world (four, if space-time is included) would be totally unaware of. Our universe could be analogous to a bubble floating with an almost infinite number of other bubble universes. Since a universe is generally thought to be everything, multiple universes are called multiverse. In any case, this is all beyond my job level. But understandable information on the subject is readily available on the internet. Interestingly, if science can explain the cause of our Big Bang, it means that time was already in existence when the Bang occurred.

Also, recall Dr. Schwartz' statement that indicated science has yet to explain the origin of human consciousness in physical terms. In fact, science by the process of evolution, has explained the origin of the species and their related structures that contain life, but has not solved the origin of life itself, particularly, intelligent awareness – no matter how well evolution theory explains the ongoing development of the myriad of species. There presently is no real science that excludes God or an eternal, absolute principle in the universe that is the first cause of all creation.

The friction between science and religion centers on facts vs. synthetic facts. Scientists deal in facts derived from nature observed in physical terms. Religionists tend to factualize ideas from an invisible realm, then state those ideas as absolute facts, usually admixing facts of physical phenomena into those ideas. Thus, the facts of science are more reliable than those of religion. Science facts have forced changes in religious views. A great example is seen in Creationism's unquestioned biblical acceptance of a 6,000-year-old earth. After scientific facts disagreed, some creationists posited a much older earth. Of course, most did not reject the Bible's accuracy, but justified the change with two new positions.

One views the days of creation as geological time periods and adjusts each day's time frame to correspond with scientific data. The other solution is known as the gap theory. A supposed gap is placed between the first and second verse of Genesis. The first verse says God created the heavens and the earth, while the second says the earth was a formless void. With a stretch of imagination, this gap is interpreted as a great period of time between the original creation and God giving form to the earth. I am not aware of any purely religious view that has forced a change to any scientific fact.

I shall now explore Genesis and science a little more. Genesis gives some detail on God's forming the earth and its habitation, including humans, over a six day period. As He also created the heavens, sun, moon, and stars, during this time we may assume the creation of the entire universe. From a scientific perspective this information is fatally flawed. For example, on the third day of creation, Genesis has vegetation growing on the earth; since this occurs the day before the sun, moon and stars are created, this indicated that the earth is the oldest physical body in the universe. Additionally, vegetation is thriving before sunlight exists. Science's facts say the universe is at least three times, or about 9 billion years older, than the earth, also, that plants must have sunlight to grow. Regardless of the length of each day, or insertion of the gap theory, these simple problems still exist.

The Zondervan Corporation's revised copyright 2000 edition of the *King James* version, says this in *About the Bible*: that Genesis was written during Moses' time, that different authors at different time periods wrote the books of the Bible: and "Yet not one of these writers contradicts another." God guided them to say in their own words what He wanted them to say. Thus, the Bible is completely dependable and we can believe every word because "it comes from God."

With time and effort one could find numerous biblical contradictions, but I have previously mentioned enough to support the point that it is plainly untrue that not one of the Bible writers contradicts another. This fact remains even if one is able to overlook the contradictions due to acceptance of some supposed experts' explanation. Yet the opening text of a Bible that was revised and published in the twenty-first century continues this false teaching. When truth is based on factualized ideas that are not supported by evidence, then is fixed in stone, with no compromise regardless of any new evidence presented, then such a truth is simply false.

Many religious people depend on faith instead of evidence without any awareness of a distinction between faith in their individual understanding of a particular religious institution's teachings and how their truth is normally arrived at in non-religious matters. It is just as false to deny contradictions in the Bible as it is for the President of any country to deny the Holocaust.

Once any factualized idea is defended at all costs regardless of contrary evidence, imagination replaces evidence. Science originates in imagination, but survives only with dependable physical facts. Much of religion originates in imagination and grows into a lot of imagination. Perhaps imagination is our only tool to really explore a personal ultimate principle of the universe, or does God really communicate with chosen individuals? Science will continue to enlighten us on the impersonal nature of the universe's laws. Could that mean that an Intelligent Designer did such an efficient job of ordering those laws that they are perceived by the human brain as impersonal? But what about a brave soul, like Schwartz, who attempts to frame an intelligent G.O.D. process by the rules of science? Surely, that is a direction that may reduce religious and scientific friction. That is not to say that friction will likely increase within the scientific community as the many scientists that oppose an "Intelligent Ordering Process" put more emphasis on defending that view. If each side adheres to the methods of science, ultimately the facts should settle the matter – at least, the issue of the validity of Dr. Schwartz' evidence and assumptions.

Probably, Schwartz' idea of God proving His own existence through science would not be as effective and certainly not as immediate as a present day miracle. Schwartz posits an Intelligent, Ordering Universal process. If this process feels the need to prove its existence, why not, for example, organize huge letters across the sky with a message that could be seen and understood around the world that says "I Am God"? Precisely because neither science nor secular history, has ever been able to document an event outside physical causation is why many believe all the incredible events described in the Bible – such as the parting of the Red Sea, or the truly dead returning to life – originated in human imagination.

Does this mean we should end our search for an eternal personal Principle that may never be found, or cannot order survival after death of human consciousness? Definitely not! Hinduism at its core has it right. Even 330 million forms or views about God cannot overcome the inherent mystery that God contains.

What do other scientifically trained, open-minded authors who promote spirit ideas, have to say?

7 SCIENCE AND SPIRIT

Deepak Chopra is a medically trained doctor that has authored a long list of successful books and related informational products. His main theme is science and spirit. Chopra is a native of India and is a master at mixing Hindu tradition with present-day reality. His formulas include the mystical and the practical in addressing healing for body, mind and spirit. Most folks may find it difficult to separate scientific fact from Chopra's mystical hypostasis.

In 2006 his text *Life After Death* was published. It carries the subtitle, *The Burden of Proof*. The opening pages include praise for this work from almost fifty prominent people.

Dr. Chopra begins his book with a *Memoir: The Life Beyond*. He tells us that as a child he viewed the hereafter, not as a place, but as a state of awareness, which he points out is contrary to the Western hereafter that is thought to be a place similar to the material world.

He says that everything we experience in this world is just consciousness expressing itself at one specific frequency and that different planes or frequencies exist simultaneously elsewhere in space-time. He says that no one frequency replaces any of the others. They all exist simultaneously; however, we experience "only what we see." After we die, we experience frequencies of finer vibrations expressed in consciousness. "Just as there are different planes of material things, there are also different spiritual planes." In fact, the number of planes or frequencies is said to be almost infinite. All planes were ultimately imagined by spirit, even in our material world.

Chopra, in the Indian tradition, says spirit is Brahman, which he explains as "everything, the one consciousness that fills every plane of existence." He further advises it can be called God or other names. "The important thing wasn't the name, but the concept of a single consciousness that creates everything and continues to do so in infinite dimensions at infinite speed."

If everything is created and maintained in the imagination of a single consciousness known as Brahman, then it is understandable how Hindus view the material world as illusion. The only reality would be the one ultimate spirit – Brahman. Does that fit with my previous exploration of the personal and the impersonal in relation to Brahman?

In the common view of Brahman being impersonal, there appears to be a conflict in its remaining that way if personal souls of enlightened humans merge eternally with Brahman. Chopra tells us that Brahman is one consciousness that fills everything in the universe as well as in the spirit world – also known as the astral world. So, in this view, Brahman is unquestionably conscious or aware. How then does one reconcile an impersonal consciousness? I suppose, something can be completely aware of events without having any attachment or regard as to how any event unfolds, which would include how creatures behave. It seems Brahman must be absolutely neutral about everything.

Buddha's famous idea of escaping all desire – not having any attachment to anything – appears to agree about neutrality. However, Buddha's thought that ultimate enlightenment is the cessation of all consciousness would nullify a Brahman with eternal consciousness; that is, unless it could be accepted that the one ultimate Spirit never becomes fully enlightened – at least, not in the Buddhist version of *nirvana*. Then again, in the Hindu view, what was human consciousness prior to reaching *nirvana* requires oneness with Brahman to finalize enlightenment. Perhaps the Brahman never becomes fully enlightened and continues to imagine new things and events throughout eternity. By extension when the consciousness of a soul that thinks and reasons in personal terms, merges with the Brahman, that soul becomes fully aware of everything that the Brahman previously experienced without having any regard or attachment to any of this newly-acquired information. In this sense, perhaps an impersonal consciousness can be superior to a personal consciousness. The trick being to have full awareness about everything previously experienced without having any concern or regard for anything. Thus, throughout eternity, the Brahman could merge with souls that had reached the highest stage of personal insight and together their one consciousness could imagine new experiences while being impersonal or neutral about anything that unfolds. I should make clear that Buddha had no need to justify anything about Brahman since it is a Hindu concept.

Consider an impersonal consciousness defined as one that has no concern for anything. It is totally devoid of feelings or emotions, yet it is totally aware of itself and everything else – that is, if we can say that there really is anything else. Chopra says Brahman (meaning spirit) imagined everything. This supports the idea of Brahman being the only reality. This concept is not that different from the biblical idea that God is the word that spoke all creation into existence. Brahman imagined and continues to imagine all reality, whereas God spoke all creation into reality and continues to maintain it. The big difference is an impersonal Brahman as opposed to a very personal God Who has great concern for event and creatures, particularly human behavior. Brahman is said to have imagined personal gods that interfaced with events and humans, but being devoid of feelings or emotions, spirit has no attachment to outcomes.

This presents the question: is Brahman intelligent? Webster gives a definition of intelligence as: capacity for learning, reasoning, and understanding; aptitude in grasping truths, relationships, facts, meaning, etc. Perhaps Brahman cannot be explained in these terms, particularly if Brahman imagined Webster and his dictionary as a reality.

Maybe it would be best to think of Brahman in terms of a conscious computer, with its software programmed with all the information that is or can ever be. The consciousness aspect of this computer is able to mix infinite information into any and all forms, events, universes, or other possibilities. Just as computers we are familiar with, this Brahman concept always remains completely neutral to the information it produces. One could argue that computers receive their information from an intelligent source, but that returns us to the age-old problem of explaining the origin of that intelligence – be it called God, Brahman, Allah, or whoever – the end point remains a choice between "God is" or "nature is." So I shall leave Brahman for other spiritual seekers to wrestle with in any of its 330 million disguises.

It should be noted that I only touched on a few pages from the beginning of Chopra's book before I once again began exploring the Brahman. Chopra goes into great detail about the hereafter and includes scientific examples as support. This is a very interesting and worthwhile read even for those who may have difficulty with some of its concepts.

A very short summary about the hereafter from *Life After Death* in my perception goes like this: one consciousness consisting of almost infinite planes is ultimately the only reality. This consciousness vibrates at all times and on all planes. These vibrations produce perceived reality in relation to their frequency. It is the thought or imagination of the one reality that produces everything – including us. On our world, the frequencies or vibrations are very dense and thus produce material reality. Science supports that all material objects are actually made of invisible vibrations. After we die and cast off this dense human body, our soul vibrates at a finer frequency on the astral (spiritual) planes, all the while continuing to experience in consciousness the perceived reality being dependent on the plane of attunement. The finer the vibration, the higher the plane that is experienced. On the astral planes, to some degree, the material planes, our thought or imagination creates whatever we desire. It is only a matter of focusing our attention. At some point during our astral journey, we pick our parents and reincarnate within the physical world – that is, until we reach the final stage of personal experience and merge with the one ultimate consciousness of all creation from whose imagination we first came. Chopra plainly believes that all of our experience has been the imagination of Brahman acting through us. Everyone has always had his awareness as a part of the whole consciousness of all creation.

Chopra offers near death experience as a possible proof of the hereafter. He mentions a Dr. Pim Van Lommel, a Dutch cardiologist who conducted a major study of near death experience. According to the study the patients had full-blown near death experience after their brains had ceased any activity – they were flat-lined until revived. This astonished Dr. Lommel. Dr. Chopra says about near death experiences, "they assure us that time may end, but consciousness continues." In another place, Chopra states that the brain stopped functioning before the near death experience began. I don't think this reflects good science. Is there an alternate explanation?

A valid one is given in the first chapter of this book, namely, "no one can say if what was recalled happened before the brain was void of activity or after the brain became active again, before the patients became fully conscious." In fact, support for this alternate possibility, can be found in Chopra's own book. On page nine, where he talks of someone dying that experiences the phenomenon of seeing their life flash by in a split second. In the same way a near death experience could also occur within a split second before the brain became inactive or a second or so before the patient came to. The near death experience then being simply recalled from normal memory, similar to a dream. Based solely on near death experience, skepticism appears appropriate regarding consciousness being independent of the brain or telling us anything about the hereafter. Still, Chopra factually states on page 241 that science "cannot explain the emergence of consciousness in the brain," which is confirmation of Dr. Schwartz in the previous chapter of this book.

Our next author deals with science and spirit in terms more familiar to the American mind. Karl W. Giberson is professor of physics at Eastern Nazarene College and directs the Forum on Faith and Science at Gordon College. He has written several books dealing with science and spirit. His *Saving Darwin* is subtitled *How To Be A Christian and Believe In Evolution*. In the introduction he tells us about his spiritual journey from a teenage, devout creationist to a scientifically educated and believing evolutionist. But for professor Giberson to believe in evolution does not mean the rejection of faith in God as the Creator or Maintainer of the universe. Instead, creation required billions of years, not six days.

Giberson says he lost confidence in the Genesis story of creation as well as the scientific creationism that attempts to place Genesis' story within the framework of modern science. But he does not see how evolution excludes God as Creator. In my humble opinion, neither do I.

He points out that creation is a secondary doctrine for Christians. The central idea being Jesus Christ and the claim that He was the Son of God. As to Jesus' incarnation, he says "thinking Christians everywhere struggle with this belief and what it means." And that "it didn't take Darwin to make Christianity offensive, complex, and intellectually challenging." He does not see Christian beliefs as being threatened by Darwin's evolution, even though he sees evolution posing two challenges to secondary Christian beliefs: this is, the fall and the uniqueness of humankind.

Giberson elegantly informs us on creationism and intelligent design and finds their teaching unacceptable. Yet he has no problem with being a Christian and accepting Darwin's evolution. He believes that Christ's resurrection offers us hope for eternal life and unity with God.

Many modern Christians have made their peace with Darwin and think that the Bible cannot be read literally as a factual book about creation. They understand that some of the biblical stories are just that – stories that contain few or no actual facts. From my observation, most thoughtful Christians have a more difficult time questioning any biblical disclosures about Jesus and the New Testament than they do with hard sayings in the Old Testament.

For answers to why science trumps the various creationists' and intelligent designers' arguments, read *Saving Darwin*.

Our final author in this chapter is Dr. Francis S. Collins, author of *The Language of God*. He is considered to be one of the world's leading scientists and was head of the human genome project. His book has the secondary title of *A Scientist Presents Evidence for Belief*. Dr. Collins' spiritual journey began in a childhood that excluded an important part for faith. His book reveals that on entering college he had become an agnostic. While pursuing a scientific education, he says: "I gradually shifted from agnosticism to atheism." At age 26 a conversation with one of his patients triggered thoughts about God.

The writings of C. S. Lewis soon put him on the path to belief. Lewis' idea of the "moral law" being a "universal feature of human existence" had a powerful influence on Dr. Collins. The latter's book invokes it many times. On page 23 he has it approaching the status of a physical law, such as, gravitation. While pointing out that it is broken with astounding regularity, he then explores if this sense of right and wrong is an intrinsic human quality. It ultimately led him to come down on the side of God's existence. He also accepted that the tools of science would not prove belief of God. That belief must be based on faith, not scientific proof. He questions if the moral law causes the "sensation of longing for something greater than ourselves." Is it "a signpost placed deep within the human spirit pointing toward something much grander than ourselves?" As opposed to a "combination of neurotransmitters landing on precisely the right receptors, setting off an electrical discharge deep within some part of the brain."

Chapter seven of Collins' book deals with atheism and agnosticism. He concludes that "science cannot be used to justify discounting the great monotheistic religions of the world." In chapter eight he reveals problems with creationism, as he also does with Intelligent Design teachings in chapter nine. Interestingly, on page 175, Collins gives us a plain view of his biblical stand. He says "parts of the Bible that are written as eyewitness accounts of historical events, including much of the New Testament" a believer ought to take these "as the writer intended – as descriptions of observed facts." Other sections of the Bible, like "the first few chapters of Genesis, the Book of Job, the Song of Solomon and the Psalms, have a more lyrical and allegorical flavor, and do not generally seem to carry the marks of pure historical narrative." For Collins, "the intention of the Bible was (and is) to reveal the nature of God to humankind."

Here, again, Collins like other scientific-accepting Christians, is more prone to take the New Testament literally as opposed to much of the Old Testament. On page 48 in a subchapter on miracles, he mentions the Old Testament event about the sun standing still and the New Testament's most significant miracle, that of Christ's resurrection from death. But he never fully explains how he deals with these events. He believes in a very low possibility for miracles as an answer to most material events. Once again, he turns to C.S. Lewis who explains the rarity of miracles that "come on great occasions: they are found at the great ganglions of history," meaning, "spiritual history which cannot be fully known by men." In chapter eleven, Collins plainly accepts Jesus as Savior and His resurrection as a fact. But he never clarifies his position on the sun and moon standing still as described in Joshua 10:12-13. Thousands of people from the Israelites' army as well as their enemy the Amorites would have been eye-witnesses to this scientifically impossible event. Joshua was the leader of the

Israelites and it was he that asked God for help in prolonging the daylight. Joshua is also credited with writing the biblical book that places this amazing event into history.

I wonder if Dr. Collins thinks these Old Testament witnesses have the same credibility as the New Testament ones that witnessed dead saints coming out of their graves and going into Jerusalem. Many thoughtful Christians probably reject both events as factual, while fully accepting all biblical accounts of Jesus' resurrection. Notwithstanding that, the four gospels vary on the details and two gospel authors – Mark and Luke – are not thought to have eye-witnessed any part of it.

Jews and Christians alike accept the Bible as God's word to humankind. However, the majority of these believers do not see all the Bible as unquestioned, literal truth. Even literalists see many passages as figures of speech, such as, allegory, metaphors, or having symbolic status meant to convey various messages. Many believers recognize that certain sayings must be relegated to the times in which they were written and may not have the same relevance today. Some are open-minded enough to recognize that the Bible is not always an adequate guide to judge other religious beliefs.

Those who approach Bible interpretation open-mindedly, can still see the Bible as inspired by God without thinking that it actually is the work of God – saying just what he wanted. The Bible writers can be seen as being so passionate about God that their natural imagination produced many thoughts of which some were written down and through acceptance by others became holy text. That they were inspired by God, at least thoughts about God would be true, but that does not mean all their thoughts or writings are true. This could well be the sense in which Paul or the author of second Timothy 3:16 meant when he wrote: "all scripture is inspired by God and is useful for teaching, for reproof, for correction and for training in righteousness."

Note that he says all scripture is "useful" (*King James* reads, "profitable"), rather than it is absolutely true. Those who continue to bog down in a literal, absolute truth from God view of the Bible, will go on deceiving themselves as well as others.

This manifests in such silly projects as creationists' promoting man and the dinosaurs as contemporaries. To show how man and prehistoric animals co-existed, maybe their theme parks and museums could rely on cartoons about Fred Flintstone.

Surely Collins and many other believing scientists possess greater minds than I do. But even their brilliant intellect is subject to bog down in unscientific thinking when it comes to God or the Bible. Few minds exceed the superior intelligence of Deepak Chopra who happens to walk a different spiritual path than Christians. Yet most prominent Christians would reject Chopra and other great Hindu teachers with one word – pantheism – defined by Webster as "the doctrine that God is the transcendent reality of which the material world and humanity are only manifestations." Curiously, the mystical side of Judaism known as kabbala, (there are other spellings) agrees with some Hindu teachings. Such as that of reincarnation and the universal consciousness that fills everything which kabbalists call *ohr ain sof*. Even though most kabbalists would deny a Hindu connection, I suspect that much of kabbala originated from Indian tradition long before Indians were Hindus, which incidentally, did not originate as a religious term, but was a designation of the Indian people by non-Indians or foreigners.

Thus, Deepak Chopra, Karl W. Giberson and Francis Collins have all shed some light on the subject of science and spirit, even if it was not definitive nor furnishing the ultimate truth, which may lie beyond man's ability to know.

Most scientists accept an evolutionary process that led to the appearance of human beings. The Bible story of the first man and woman being created full grown and talking is not accepted as factual by most scientifically oriented people.

The next chapter is devoted to an evolutionary creation of humans that credits a spiritual source.

8 AN ALTERNATE CREATION

Consider a view of human creation that includes evolution and allows the possibility of God as the First Cause. However, the evolution portrayed occurs much faster than that accepted by science. I shall return to *The Urantia Book* and let it tell its story of Andon and Fonta, the first human occupants of the earth, not to be confused with Adam and Eve who are real beings in *The Urantia Book*. But they do not arrive in human history until over 955,000 years after the first two humans.

Recall that *The Urantia Book* portrays trillions of inhabited worlds in the universe of universes. On page 399, it says:

> Life does not spontaneously appear in the universe. The Life Carriers must initiate it on the barren planets. They are the carriers, disseminators, and guardians of life as it appears on the evolutionary worlds of space. All life of the order and forms known on Urantia arises with these sons, though not all forms of planetary life are existent on Urantia.

These Life Carriers often carry an actual life plasm to a planet. But sometimes they formulate the life plasm from that planet's organic raw materials, which was the case of our earth.

In connection with spiritual and super-physical forces, the Life Carriers organized and initiated these life patterns by planting them in hospitable waters on earth. There were three identical, original marine-life implantations. No life process began before our planet had obtained a suitable evolutionary state.

The process of evolution brings us to the *Dawn Races of Early Man*, which is the title of Paper 62 in *The Urantia Book*. It tells us:

> About one million years ago the intermediate ancestors of mankind made their appearance by three successive and sudden mutations stemming from early stock of the lemur type of placental mammal. The dominant factors of these early lemurs were derived from the western or later American group of the evolving life plasm. But before establishing the direct line of human ancestry, this strain was reinforced by contributions from the central life implantation evolved from Africa. The eastern life group contributed little or nothing to the actual production of the human species.

THE EARLY LEMUR TYPES

The early lemurs concerned in the ancestry of the human species were not directly related to the pre-existent tribes of gibbons and apes then living in Eurasia and northern Africa, whose progeny have survived to the present time. Neither were they the offspring of the modern type of lemur, though springing from an ancestor common to both but long since extinct.

While these early lemurs evolved in the Western hemisphere, the establishment of the direct mammalian ancestry of mankind took place in southwestern Asia, in the original area of the central life implantation but on the borders of the eastern regions. Several million years ago the North American type lemurs had migrated westward over the Bering land bridge and had slowly made their way southwestward along the Asiatic coast. These migrating tribes finally reached the salubrious region lying between the then expanded Mediterranean Sea and the elevating mountainous regions of the Indian peninsula. In these lands to the west of India they united with other and favorable strains, thus establishing the ancestry of the human race.

With the passing of time the seacoast of India southwest of the mountains gradually submerged, completely isolating the life of this region. There was no avenue of approach to, or escape from, this Mesopotamian or Persian peninsula except to the north, and that was repeatedly cut off by the southern invasions of the glaciers. And it was in this then almost paradisiacal area, and from the superior descendants of this lemur type of mammal, that there sprang two great groups, the simian tribes of modern times and the present-day human species.

THE DAWN MAMMALS

A little more than one million years ago the Mesopotamian dawn mammals, the direct descendants of the North American lemur type of placental mammal, suddenly appeared. They were active little creatures, almost three feet tall; and while they did not habitually walk on their hind legs, they could easily stand erect. They were hairy and agile and chattered in monkeylike fashion, but unlike the simian tribes, they were flesh eaters. They had a primitive opposable thumb as well as a highly useful grasping big toe. From this point onward the prehuman species successively developed the opposable thumb while they progressively lost the grasping power of the great toe. The later ape tribes retained the grasping big toe, but never developed the human type of thumb.

These dawn mammals attained full growth when three or four years of age, having a potential life span, on the average, of about twenty years. As a rule, offspring were born singly, although twins were occasional.

The members of this new species had the largest brains for their size of any animal that had theretofore existed on earth. They experienced many of the emotions and shared numerous instincts which later characterized primitive man, being highly curious and exhibiting considerable elation when successful at any undertaking. Food hunger and sex craving were well developed and a definite sex selection was manifested in a crude form of courtship and choice of mates. They would fight fiercely in defense of their kindred and were quite tender in family associations, possessing a sense of self-abasement bordering on shame and remorse. They were very affectionate and touchingly loyal to their mates, but if circumstances separated them, they would choose new partners.

Being of small stature and having keen minds to realize the dangers of their forest habitat, they developed an extraordinary fear which led to those wise precautionary measures that so enormously contributed to survival, such as their construction of crude shelters in the high tree tops which eliminated many of the perils of ground life. The beginning of the fear tendencies of mankind more specifically dates from these days.

These dawn mammals developed more of a tribal spirit than had ever been previously exhibited. They were, indeed, highly gregarious but nevertheless exceedingly pugnacious when in any way disturbed in the ordinary pursuit of their routine life, and they displayed fiery tempers when their anger was fully aroused. Their bellicose natures, however, served a good purpose; superior groups did not hesitate to make war on their inferior neighbors, and thus, by selective survival, the species was progressively improved. They very soon dominated the life of the smaller creatures of the region, and very few of the older carnivorous monkeylike tribes survived.

These aggressive little animals multiplied and spread over the Mesopotamian peninsula for more than one thousand years, constantly improving in physical type and general intelligence. And it was just seventy generations after this new tribe had taken origin from the highest type of lemur ancestor that the next epoch-making development occurred – the sudden differentiation of the ancestors of the next vital step in the evolution of human beings on Urantia.

THE MID-MAMMALS

Early in the career of the dawn mammals, in the treetop abode of a superior pair of these agile creatures, twins were born, one male and one female. Compared with their ancestors, they were really handsome little creatures. They had little hair on their bodies, but this was no disability as they lived in a warm and equable climate.

These children grew to be a little over four feet in height. They were in ever way larger than their parents, having longer legs and shorter arms. They had almost perfectly opposable thumbs, just about as well adapted for diversified work as the present human thumb. They walked upright, having feet almost as well suited for walking as those of the later human races.

Their brains were inferior to, and smaller than, those of human beings but very superior to, and comparatively much larger than, those of their ancestors. The twins early displayed superior intelligence and were soon recognized as the heads of the whole tribe of dawn mammals, really instituting a primitive form of social organization and a crude economic division of labor. This brother and sister mated and soon enjoyed the society of twenty-one children much like themselves, all more than four feet tall and in every way superior to the ancestral species. This new group formed the nucleus of the mid-mammals.

When the numbers of this new and superior group grew great, war, relentless war, broke out; and when the terrible struggle was over, not a single individual of the pre-existent and ancestral race of dawn mammals remained alive. The less numerous but more powerful and intelligent offshoot of the species had survived at the expense of their ancestors.

And now, for almost fifteen thousand years (six hundred generations), this creature became the terror of this part of the world. All of the great and vicious animals of former times had perished. The large beasts native to these regions were not carnivorous, and the larger species of the cat family, lions and tigers, had not yet invaded this peculiarly sheltered nook of the earth's surface. Therefore did these mid-mammals wax valiant and subdue the whole of their corner of creation.

Compared with the ancestral species, the mid-mammals were an improvement in every way. Even their potential life span was longer, being about twenty-five years. A number of rudimentary human traits appeared in this new species. In addition to the innate propensities exhibited by their ancestors, these mid-mammals were capable of showing disgust in certain repulsive situations. They further possessed a well-defined hoarding instinct; they would hide food for subsequent use and were greatly given to the collection of smooth round pebbles and certain types of round stones suitable for defensive and offensive ammunition.

These mid-mammals were the first to exhibit a definite construction propensity, as shown in their rivalry in the building of both treetop homes and their many-tunneled subterranean retreats; they were the first species of mammals ever to provide for safety in both arboreal and underground shelters. They largely forsook the trees as places of abode, living on the ground during the day and sleeping in the treetops at night.

As time passed, the natural increase in numbers eventually resulted in serious food competition and sex rivalry, all of which culminated in a series of internecine battles that nearly destroyed the entire species. These struggles continued until only one group of less than one hundred individuals was left alive. But peace once more prevailed, and this lone surviving tribe built anew its treetop bedrooms and again resumed a normal and semi-peaceful existence.

You can hardly realize by what narrow margins your prehuman ancestors missed extinction from time to time. Had the ancestral frog of all humanity jumped two inches less on a certain occasion, the whole course of evolution would have been markedly changed. The intermediate lemurlike mother of the dawn-mammal species escaped death no less than five times by mere hairbreath margins before she gave birth to the father of the new and higher mammalian order. But the closest call of all when lightning struck the tree in which the prospective mother of the Primates twins was sleeping. Both of these mid-mammals parents were severely shocked and badly burned; three of their seven children were killed by this bolt from the skies. These evolving animals were almost superstitious. The couple whose treetop home had been struck were really the leaders of the more progressive group of the mid-mammals species; and following their example, more than half the tribe embracing the more intelligent families, moved about two miles away from this locality and began the construction of new treetop abodes and new ground shelters – their transient retreats in time of sudden danger.

Modern man and the simians did spring from the same tribe and species but not from the same parents. Man's ancestors are descended from the superior strains of the selected remnant of this mid-mammal tribe, whereas the modern simians (excepting certain pre-existent types of lemurs, gibbons, apes, and other monkeylike creatures) are the descendants of the most inferior couple of this mid-mammal group, a couple who only survived by hiding themselves in a subterranean food-storage retreat for more than two weeks during the last fierce battle of their tribe, emerging only after the hostilities were well over.

Going back to the birth of the superior twins, one male and one female, to the two leading members of the mid-mammal tribe: these animal babies were of an unusual order; they had still less hair on their bodies than their parents and, when very young, insisted on walking upright. Their ancestors had always learned to walk on their hind legs, but these Primates twins stood erect from the beginning. They attained a height of over five feet, and their heads grew larger in comparison with others in the tribe. While early learning to communicate with each other by means of signs and symbols, they were never able to make their people understand these new symbols.

When about fourteen years of age, they fled from the tribe, going west to raise their family and establish the new species of Primates. And these new creatures are very properly denominated Primates since they were the direct and immediate animal ancestors of the human family itself.

Thus it was that the Primates came to occupy a region on the west coast of the Mesopotamian peninsula as it then projected into the southern sea, while the less intelligent and closely related tribes lived around the peninsula point and up to the eastern shore line.

The Primates were more human and less animal than their mid-mammal predecessors. The skeletal proportions of this new species were very similar to those of the primitive human races. The human type of hand and foot had fully developed, and these creatures could walk and even run as well as any of their later-day human descendants. They largely abandoned tree life, though continuing to resort to the treetops as a safety measure at night, for like their earlier ancestors, they were greatly subject to fear. The increased use of their hands did much to develop inherent brain power, but they did not yet possess minds that could really be called human.

Although emotional in nature the Primates differed little from their forebears; they exhibited more of a human trend in all of their propensities. They were, indeed, splendid and superior animals, reaching maturity at about ten years of age and having a natural life span of about forty years. That is, they might have lived that long had they died natural deaths, but in those early days very few animals ever died a natural death; the struggle for existence was altogether too intense.

And now, after almost nine hundred generations of development, covering about twenty-one thousand years from the origin of the dawn mammals, the Primates suddenly gave birth to two remarkable creatures, the first true human beings.

Thus it was that the dawn mammals, springing from the North American lemur type, gave origin to the mid-mammals, and these mid-mammals in turn produced the superior Primates, who became the immediate ancestors of the primitive human race. The Primates tribes were the last vital link in the evolution of man, but in less than five thousand years not a single individual of these extraordinary tribes was left.

THE FIRST HUMAN BEINGS

From the year 1934 back to the birth of the first human beings is just 993,419 years.

These two remarkable creatures were true human beings. They possessed perfect human thumbs, as had many of their ancestors, while they had just as perfect feet as the present-day human races. They were walkers and runners, not climbers; the grasping function of the big toe was absent, completely absent. When danger drove them to the treetops, they climbed just like the humans of today would. They would climb up the trunk of a tree like a bear and not as would a chimpanzee or a gorilla, swinging by the branches.

The first human beings (and their descendants) reached maturity at twelve years of age and possessed a potential life span of about seventy-five years.

Many new emotions early appeared in these human twins. They experienced admiration for both objects and other beings and exhibited considerable vanity. But the most remarkable advance in emotional development was the sudden appearance of a new group of really human feelings, the worshipful group, embracing awe, reverence, humility and even a primitive form of gratitude. Fear, joined with ignorance of natural phenomena, is about to give birth to primitive religion.

Not only were such human feelings manifested in these primitive humans, but many more highly evolved sentiments were also present in rudimentary form. They were mildly cognizant of pity, shame, and reproach and were acutely conscious of love, hate, revenge, being also susceptible to marked feelings of jealousy.

These first two humans – the twins – were a great trial to their Primates parents. They were so curious and adventurous that they nearly lost their lives on numerous occasions before they were eight years old. As it was, they were rather well scarred up by the time they were twelve.

Very early they learned to engage in verbal communication; by the age of ten they had worked out an improved sign and word language of almost half a hundred ideas and had greatly improved and expanded the crude communicative technique of their ancestors. But try as hard as they might, they were able to teach only a few of their new signs and symbols to their parents.

When about nine years of age, they journeyed down the river one bright day and held a momentous conference. Every celestial intelligence stationed on Urantia, including myself, was present as an observer of the transactions of this noontime tryst. On this eventful day they arrived at an understanding to live for and with each other, and this was the first of a series of such agreements which finally culminated in the decision to flee from their inferior animal associates and to journey northward, little knowing that they were thus to found the human race.

While we were all greatly concerned with what these two little savages were planning, we were powerless to control the working of their minds; we did not – could not – arbitrarily influence their decisions. But within the limits of permissible planetary function, we, the Life Carriers, together with our associates, all conspired to lead the human twins northward and far from their hairy and partially tree-dwelling people. And so, by reason of their own intelligent choice, the twins did migrate, and because of our supervision they migrated northward to a secluded region where they escaped the possibility of biological degradation through admixture with their inferior relatives of the Primates tribes.

Shortly before their departure from the home forests they lost their mother in a gibbon raid. While she did not possess their intelligence, she did have a worthy mammalian affection of a high order for her offspring, and she fearlessly gave her life in the attempt to save the wonderful pair. Nor was her sacrifice in vain, for she held off the enemy until the father arrived with reinforcements and put the raiders to rout. Soon after this young couple forsook their associates to found the human race, their Primates father became disconsolate – he was heartbroken. He refused to eat, even when food was brought to him by his other children. His brilliant offspring having been lost, life did not seem worth living among his ordinary fellows, so he wandered off into the forest and was set upon by hostile gibbons and beaten to death.

These first two human twins were named Andon and Fonta by the chief of the archangel corps. The bulk of Urantia Paper 62 has herein been disclosed as it was narrated by a Life

Carrier of Nebadon who is said to have resided on our planet for over 500 million years.

Nothing in our present day science supports the existence of any of the numerous supernatural beings described in *The Urantia Book*; however, some scientists have suggested that life on earth may have been seeded from outer space. A few mavericks have proposed the possibility that life may have been brought here by alien beings. But the majority of scientists that entertain the possibility of life on earth being seeded from space think that germs or bacteria or some organic compound came in a natural vehicle, such as comets or meteors.

The interesting aspect about so-called supernatural beings, such as Life Carriers – if they actually do exist – then they are just a natural part of the universe that we have been ignorant of. As previously mentioned, the First Cause – if accepted as God – would be the most natural thing there is.

Next to other possibilities about God.

GOD

In Chapter Seven I suggested that a brilliant scientist such as Dr. Collins could bog down in unscientific thinking when it came to God or the Bible. But in all fairness to Collins, I had already said that he believed that God must be based on faith rather than scientific proof. Of course, faith absent of physical evidence is unscientific.

It appears that one's faith must include an element of imagination that says I know God is real because I just know. But what shapes that knowing? It is mostly the association of an individual with a religious institution or teacher whose wisdom is generally based on holy texts or holy tradition.

Most of the time one's religious preference is the product of his or her childhood environment. That does not necessarily mean that the child as an adult follows the religion of the parents or of his earliest religious exposure. In some cases, due to negative thoughts or experiences with the parents' religion, or experience with different religious teachings, grown children choose another religious path or may reject religion altogether. As seen in the examples of both Karl Giberson and Dr. Collins, one's education can play a major role in shaping one's own belief.

Others may stay active in a chosen religious institution primarily as a traditional or societal function. I don't think that the majority of active religious adherents give much thought to the truth of their beliefs. Rather, truth is assumed and more thought pertains to making the evidence fit that truth or rejecting evidence that tends to disagree without honestly evaluating it.

In any case, I think it is safe to say most people think that God is real because their religion says so. There is also the possibility that a Thought Adjustor as related in *The Urantia Book* influences the human mind in that direction. In fact, many Christians accept that God in the form of the Holy Spirit affects minds that way. Be it called The Holy Spirit or the Thought Adjustor, either is essentially seen to be a part of God.

But how did religion get started in the first place? It seems the idea of God or gods had first to develop in human imagination before religion would have been needed to explain that idea.

Previously in its disclosure on the first human beings *The Urantia Book* in mentioning human emotions, states, "fear, joined with ignorance of natural phenomena is about to give birth to primitive religion."

Assume that fear and ignorance of nature were the catalysts that drove early man to believe that some invisible source or thing was the cause of his misfortunes. For example, an animal attack, a storm destroying his shelter, death of a comrade, etc. A crude idea of an animal or human-shaped being with super-physical abilities from the invisible spirit world was thought to be behind any calamity. And it would later be credited as the source of good fortune, particularly if praise or worship had been directed toward this invisible super-thing. Food or other enticements would insure benevolence from this invisible being who controlled human destiny. Man soon expressed his ideas of gods and religion in physical terms with totems, idols and ritual: that produced hymns, incantations, charms, spells, curses, sacrifices, dances and all sorts of elaborate structures and practices.

Information from Wikipedia entitled "Prehistoric Religion" tells us that intentional burial of undisputed *homo sapiens* dates back 130,000 years. This has been seen as the earliest detectable form of religious practice particularly when grave goods are included. Evidence in support of animal worship dates from circa 70,000 B.C.E. It is found in the African Kalahari desert in the form of a python-shaped rock that is accompanied by a lot of broken spear points as well as a secret chamber discovered inside a cave.

Apparently, some idea of a God or gods has been part of human thinking for a very long time. However, known written history dates to 5,000 or so years ago when cuneiform script came into use. The oldest religious writings – the pyramid texts – are Egyptian compositions that began almost 4,500 years ago. What is known about these earliest recorded practices and sayings had some effect on religion today. Texts younger than 2,000 years are the major authority of present times.

Still, current copies of the Old Testament and Hinduism's primary text the *Vedas* are said to be based on much older oral traditions which went to great length to pass them on accurately.

Judaism and Islam originated with Abraham whose time is thought to have been around 4,000 years ago. However, Hebrew did not become a written language until 1,200 or so years later. And most of the Old Testament scriptures may not have been written down until 300 or so years after that. Some parts are thought to have been composed even later. The original texts are lost to history while the oldest known copy of any part of the Old Testament is found in bits and pieces from the 2,000-year-old Dead Sea scrolls that include an almost complete copy of the Book of Isaiah. Thus, the oldest available copy of any Old Testament text is dated at least 500 years later than most of the original.

Islam took root as a religion during Mohammed's time in the seventh century C.E. Keep in mind this was perhaps over 1,000 years after the Old Testament was reduced to writing and was over 2,500 years after Abraham is thought to have had his first conversation with God. Prior to Alexander the Great's conquest of Palestine in 332 B.C.E., the Old Testament is the only known history of the Jews.

It should also be noted that Mohammed's time was some 600 years after Jesus. Not only does Islam think some of the

Old Testament contains errors, it also feels the same about the New Testament. So what basis does Islam have for disagreeing with major Biblical disclosures? The Koran! Remember, Muslims believe the Koran to be direct revelation from the angel Gabriel to Mohammed. Consider Koranic scripture 4:171 that says Jesus, the Son of Mary, was no more than a messenger of Allah. In this same verse a trinity concept of God is denied – "Allah is one God." Earlier in 4:48 the Koran says that it is an unforgivable sin to set up partners with Allah, thus meaning God has no equals.

Judaism and Islam would agree that humankind is God's children only in the sense that God originally created man and woman. Neither religion agrees with Christianity on the view that God was the Fatherly source that begat Jesus; although oddly, Islam accepts the Virgin Mary as Jesus' Mother. The Koran teaches this special birth of Jesus, but sees Him as God's messenger on a status with Moses. Judaism generally holds that, at best, Jesus was an influential Jewish rabbi or teacher Who deviated from the accepted teachings of Judaism during His ministry.

Like Islam, present day Judaism does not accept a trinity concept of God. Curiously, both the Old Testament and the Koran have passages that have God speaking of Himself in plural form. For example, Koranic scripture 2:34 and 2:35 have God speaking as "We said." Another Koranic verse, 2:60, refers to the conflicting biblical subject about Moses getting water from a rock. The Koran reads: "We said: Strike the rock with thy staff." My copy of the Koran (spelled Qur'an) was translated into English by Abdullah Yusuf Ali and in many verses has God talking in the plural.

In the second edition of *The Complete Idiot's Guide to Understanding Islam* by Yahiya Emerick, page 46 explains that when God refers to Himself as "We" or "Us" in the Koran that such plural usage of pronouns is a common technique called the "royal we" that is used in numerous languages. For example, a powerful ruler might make a decree in the plural, even though he is one person, to emphasize the concept "I and my authority" are making this decree.

While that is a common justification on this issue, it does not explain the unpredictable use of the "royal we." For example, Koranic verse 41:39 includes: "among His signs . . . We send down rain," while 42:28 prefers: "He is the one that sends down rain." Also, use of the "royal we" may now be a common technique, but were the writers of the Koran some 1400 years ago aware of this technique? What do *The KJ Study Bible* experts have to say about God speaking plurally?

Three plural verses where God refers to Himself in the Old Testament are Genesis 1:26, 3:22 and 11:7. In its first study note at Genesis 1:1 *The KJ Study Bible* says: "The Hebrew noun *Elohim* is plural, but the verb is singular, a normal usage in the Old Testament when reference is to the one true God." It further says the plural expresses intensification rather than number. Hebrew text does use the plural *Elohim* in the Bible's first verse as well as various other Old Testament verses.

However, the KJ has God in the singular in Genesis 1:1. In 1:26 God says, "Let us make man in our image after our likeness." Verse 3:22 has the Lord God saying "the man is become as one of us." Then, 11:7 states that the Lord said, "Let us go down." Not only does God speak in the plural, He is designated differently in each of these three verses – God, Lord God and Lord.

The study note on 1:26 justified "us" and "our" by explaining God as the Creator-King proclaiming His crowning work (the creation of humans) to His heavenly court. Possibly God was addressing heavenly associates such as angels, who would be acceptable to both Christian and Jewish theology. Although Islam surely believes in angels, it plainly rejects that man was made in God's image.

These explanations of God speaking in the plural, both in the Bible and the Koran, conclude that it is for the purpose of emphasis or intensification. If so, since Judaism, Christianity and Islam have always accepted God as all-knowing and all powerful, I have to wonder why God would ever need to call special attention to His authority or His act in any particular situation. With a plural concept of God as the Trinity being a major part of Catholic theology, what does the Catholic Study Bible explain on these verses? Even though the above Old Testament verses tend to support a Trinity concept, oddly my Catholic Bible ignores any commentary on the subject.

Perhaps *The Urantia Book* offers enlightenment with its information on the evolution of God's name in Jewish history. From paper 96 entitled *Yahweh – God of the Hebrews:*

> In conceiving of Deity, man first includes all gods, then subordinates all foreign gods to his tribal deity, and finally excludes all but the one God of final and supreme value. The Jews synthesized all gods into their more sublime concept of the Lord God of Israel. The Hindus likewise combined their multifarious deities into the "one spirituality of the gods" portrayed in the Rig-Veda, while the Mesopotamians reduced their gods to the more centralized concept of Bel-Marduk. These ideas of monotheism matured all over the world not long after the appearance of Machiventa Melchizedek at Salem in Palestine. But the Melchizedek concept of Deity was unlike that of the evolutionary philosophy of inclusion, subordination and exclusion: it was based exclusively on *creative power* and very soon influenced the highest deity concepts of Mesopotamia, India and Egypt.
>
> The Salem religion was revered as a tradition by the Kenites and several other Caananite tribes. And this was one of the purposes of Melchizedek's incarnation: that a religion of one God should be so fostered as to prepare the way for the earth bestowal of a Son of that one God. Michael could hardly come

to Urantia until there existed a people believing in the Universal Father among whom he could appear.

The Salem religion persisted among the Kenites in Palestine as their creed, and the religion as it was later adopted by the Hebrews was influenced, first, by Egyptian moral teachings; later, by Babylonian theologic thought; and, lastly, by Iranian conceptions of good and evil. Factually, the Hebrew religion is predicated upon the covenant between Abraham and Machiventa Melchizedek, evolutionally it is the outgrowth of many unique situational circumstances, but culturally it has borrowed freely from the religion, morality and philosophy of the entire Levant. It is through the Hebrew religion that much of the morality and religious thought of Egypt, Mesopotamia and Iran was transmitted to the Occidental peoples.

DEITY CONCEPTS AMONG THE SEMITES

The early Semites regarded everything as being indwelt by a spirit. There were spirits of the animal and vegetable worlds; annual spirits, the lord of progeny; spirits of fire, water and air; a veritable pantheon of spirits to be feared and worshipped. And the teaching of Melchizedek regarding a Universal Creator never fully destroyed the belief in these subordinate spirits or nature gods.

The progress of the Hebrews from polytheism through henotheism to monotheism was not an unbroken and continuous conceptual development. They experienced many retrogressions in the evolution of their Deity concepts, while during any one epoch there existed varying ideas of God among different groups of Semite believers. From time to time numerous terms were applied to their concepts of God and in order to prevent confusion these various Deity titles will be defined as they pertain to the evolution of Jewish theology:

1. *Yahweh* was the god of the southern Palestine tribes, who associated this concept of deity with Mount Horeb, the Sinai volcano. Yahweh was merely one of the hundreds and thousands of nature gods which held the attention and claimed the worship of the Semitic tribes and peoples.

2. *El Elyon.* For centuries after Melchizedek's sojourn at Salem his doctrine of Deity persisted in various versions but was generally connoted by the term El Elyon, the Most High God of heaven. Many Semites, including the immediate descendants of Abraham, at various times worshipped both Yahweh and El Elyon.

3. *El Shaddai.* It is difficult to explain what El Shaddai stood for. This idea of God was a composite derived from the teachings of Amenomope's Book of Wisdom modified by Ikhnaton's doctrine of Aton and further influenced by Melchizedek's teachings embodied in the concept of El Elyon. But as the concept of El Shaddai permeated the Hebrew mind, it became thoroughly colored with the Yahweh beliefs of the desert.

4. *El.* Amid all this confusion of terminology and haziness of concept, many devout believers sincerely endeavored to worship all of these evolving ideas of divinity and there grew up the practice of referring to this composite deity as El. And this term

included still other of the Bedouin nature gods.

5. *Elohim.* In Kish and Ur there long persisted Sumerian-Chaldean groups who taught a three-in-one God concept founded on the traditions of the days of Adam and Melchizedek. This doctrine was carried to Egypt, where this Trinity was worshipped under the name of Elohim, or in the singular as Eloah. The philosophic circles of Egypt and later Alexandrian teachers of Hebraic extraction taught this unity of pluralistic Gods and many of Moses' advisers at the time of the exodus believed in this Trinity, but the concept of the Trinitarian Elohim never became a real part of Hebrew theology until after they had come under the political influence of the Babylonians.

6. *Sundry names.* The Semites disliked to speak the name of their Deity and they therefore resorted to numerous appellations from time to time, such as: The Spirit of God, The Lord, The Angel of the Lord, The Almighty, The Holy One, The Most High, Adonai, The Ancient of Days, The Lord God of Israel, The Creator of Heaven and Earth, Kyrios, Jah, The Lord of Hosts and The Father in Heaven.

Jehovah is a term which in recent times has been employed to designate the completed concept of Yahweh which finally evolved in the long Hebrew experience. But the name Jehovah did not come into use until fifteen hundred years after the time of Jesus.

Up to about 2,000 B.C.E. Mount Sinai was intermittently active as a volcano, occasional eruptions occurring as late as the time of the sojourn of the

Israelites in this region. The fire and smoke, together with the thunderous detonations associated with the eruptions of this volcanic mountain, all impressed and awed the Bedouins of the surrounding regions and caused them greatly to fear Yahweh. This spirit of Mount Horeb later became the god of the Hebrew Semites and they eventually believed him to be supreme over all other gods.

The Caananites had long revered Yahweh, and although many of the Kenites believed more or less in El Elyon, the super-god of the Salem religion, a majority of the Caananites held loosely to the worship of the old tribal deities. They were hardly willing to abandon their national deities in favor of an international, not to say an interplanetary, God. They were not universal-deity minded, and therefore these tribes continued to worship their tribal deities, including *Yahweh* and the silver and golden calves which symbolized the Bedouin herders' concept of the spirit of the Sinai volcano.

The Syrians, while worshipping their gods, also believed in Yahweh of the Hebrews, for their prophets said to the Syrian king: "Their gods are gods of the hills; therefore they were stronger than we; but let us fight against them on the plain and surely we shall be stronger than they."

As man advances in culture, the lesser gods are subordinated to a supreme deity; the great Jove persists only as an exclamation. The monotheists keep their subordinate gods as spirits, demons, fates, Nereids, fairies, brownies, dwarfs, banshees and the evil eye. The Hebrews passed through henotheism and long believed in the existence of gods other than Yahweh. They conceded the actuality of Chemosh, god of the Amorites, but maintained that he was subordinate to Yahweh.

The idea of Yahweh has undergone the most extensive development of all the mortal theories of God. Its progressive evolution can only be compared with the metamorphosis of the Buddha concept in Asia, which in the end led to the concept of the Universal Absolute even as the Yahweh concept finally led to the idea of the Universal Father. But as a matter of historic fact, it should be understood that, while the Jews thus changed their views of Deity, from the tribal god of Mount Horeb to the loving and merciful Creator Father of later times, they did not change his name; they continued all the way along to call this evolving concept of Deity, Yahweh.

I should explain that according to *The Urantia Book*, the supernatural being Machiventa Melchizedek was incarnated on earth allegedly in full-grown human form. During the days of Abraham was not the first time that Machiventa and others of his type had been active on earth. He was said to be the teacher of Abraham and he maintained a religious school at Salem which today is called Jerusalem. And the Old Testament covenant between God and Abraham was really between Machiventa and Abraham.

Returning to the various names for God, the internet source Wikipedia's *Names Of God in Judaism* (March 2009) offers abundant information. Also, Wikipedia's *Elohim* (March 2009) advises that the word *Elohim's* significance is often disputed in that "there are many theories as to why the word is plural." Among them:

1. "to augment its meaning and form an abstraction meaning 'Divine Majesty'; "
2. sometimes Trinitarian Christian writing sees this as evidence for the Holy Trinity doctrine;

3. another view has the word's plurality as a reflection on early Semitic polytheism.

This source also explains *Elohim* in the Koran's use of a first person plural pronoun ("We") as implying the presence of angels. As in the Bible, when oneness of God is intended, the singular is used.

Perhaps this chapter brings into focus how the various twists of interpretation in the teaching about the God of Abraham offer such differing paths to knowing Him.

The Israelites, also known as Hebrews or Jews, originally stem from desert nomads that began to unite under the leadership of Moses. As previously noted, there is no archeological or secular historical evidence that confirms anything relating to Moses or the Exodus that is thought to have occurred about 3,200 years ago. However, within a few hundred years the Jews were factually established as a race and a religion that claimed the Israelites to be the chosen people of the mightiest God Who created heaven, earth and its occupants. By Jesus' time, the Hebrew priests had firm control over the thought and action of the Jewish people, not only as to how they related to God, but in every facet of their daily life. At the time the Jews were under Roman rule. Certain priestly decrees, such as a death penalty, required Roman approval.

The Hebrew Scriptures were the basis of priestly teaching and authority was passed on by inheritance within priestly family lines. But it would be 100 or so years after Jesus' death before these Scriptures were refined by separating those which were considered to be inspired by God from the ones that were not. The inspired ones became the Old Testament.

Christianity took root within the Jewish religion and adopted the Jewish Scriptures as authoritative. Jesus was the Inspiration for many new religious writings. In a short time Christianity broke away from Judaism and became its competitor. Although there were numerous Christian groups competing among themselves, the Catholic (universal) Church early gained dominance. In the fourth century C.E. the Roman political ruler Constantine turned to Christianity and laid the foundation for it to become the official religion of Rome. In an effort to unite Christianity and standardize its practices, thereby making it easier to control its followers, he called the first Christian conference. Its purpose was, among other things, to choose from among the numerous Christian writers, perhaps as many as 200 or more, so as to establish an official cannon of the Church. Ultimately, the 27 books we now know as the New Testament were selected. Also, some of the Hebrew Scriptures that had been rejected by Judaism for inclusion in the official Old Testament because they were not considered inspired by God were accepted by the Church. They are known as the Apocrypha and are included in Catholic Bibles as seven extra books, as well as additions to the Book of Esther. Protestant and Jewish Bibles do not include these modifications and, of course, Jewish Bibles exclude all of the New Testament.

In making a final selection for a Christian Bible over a period of many years, imagine what heated debates must have occurred among the participating clergy. Supposedly, there were arguments against including any of the Old Testament as well as strong opposition to the Book of Revelation. In any case, the decision of the fourth-century Church authorities produced the Christian Holy Bible. Three centuries later, on becoming a religion founded by Mohammed, Islam accepted the Bible as holy text, but sees it as being corrupted by some Christian and Jewish leaders. Islamicists view the Koran as the sacred word of God and fundamentalists see it as the inerrant word of God, just like most fundamental Christians' view of the Bible.

Interestingly, I came across a promotion on the internet from Prometheus Books for the title *In Search of the Original Koran: the True History of the Revealed Text*, by Mondher Sfar. The promotion says Sfar is an historian that reveals the lack of any historical or theological "basis for the Orthodox view that Muhammad or his earliest followers intended the Koran to be treated as the inviolable word of God." Sfar even points out: "passages from Islam's sacred book clearly indicate that the revealed text should not be equated with the perfect text of the original 'celestial Koran,' which was believed to exist only in heaven and to be fully known only to God." Anyone wishing to pursue this issue will find Sfar's book to be a rare source on the subject.

As regards the hereafter, the Koran repeatedly makes clear that proper allegiance to Allah will reward his followers with heavenly gardens that have rivers underneath and that eternal fiery burning will be the fate of the unfaithful. The Koran many times makes the point that God is merciful and oft forgiving.

Thus far, various extant religious belief and commentary has mostly been the subject of this book. Next I will explore God from a neutral perspective – at least, as neutral as possible.

10 THE GOD OF LOGIC

The previous chapter presents the possibility that early man created God, like many unbelievers say, as a crutch to lean on in times of hardship, as well as an object of praise when good fortune is experienced. Thus, man gradually created God or gods to conform with man's imagination.

If true, no imaginary spirit creation can order an afterlife for human beings. Evolution of God in the minds of men brings us to the present day in which religion's main tool in knowing God is found in holy texts. Notably, the Bible or the Koran are the authoritative sources to over half of the earth's population.

But what if I explore God from a logical viewpoint and try not to be influenced by existent religious ideas? Is it logical to believe in God as the First Cause of all creation? Yes! Cause and effect is an essential principle in human thinking. Everything that happens in our experience relates to an effect being the product of some cause. That does not mean that we always know the cause that produced an effect. But with effort we can usually determine the cause of most effects, at least, the immediate cause of an effect.

Consider that the mechanical pencil I first used to write this sentence had the effect to stop working. The cause was that it simply ran out of lead. If we stop right here, we know the cause and the effect relating to my pencil. However, an attempt to regress beyond this known cause of my pencil becoming inoperative results in the cause becoming an effect. In other words, the effect of my pencil having no lead could then be seen as caused by my failure to add lead to the pencil before it ran out.

The central point is that cause and effect is a normal part of human experience. And depending on the depth of exploration, cause itself may be interpreted as an effect or an effect might be seen as a cause since human thinking insists on a starting point – a beginning. Believers understood God to be the First Cause of everything while non-believers accept unguided nature as the first cause. Either view is logical, but only one is true.

Science offers sound theories and material facts as proof of nature's power, but science cannot rule out the possibility of God or an ultimate Being as the First Cause of all creation. Religion stakes its claim on proof of God mainly on the doings and sayings of long-dead people.

Even relatively modern religious sects such as Mormons or Jehovah Witnesses base their core teachings on the Bible and simply put their own twist to its sayings. In Islam, Sunni and Shiites both accept the same ancient Koran as holy text, but have their differences, sometimes expressed violently. Orthodox and Reform Jews look to the same Holy Scriptures, not necessarily the same interpretations.

Buddha first taught about 500 years before Jesus' time. Hinduism's Vedic teachings were available to Buddha, but he taught a simpler, more practical path than had been developed in Hinduism.

Is it logical that all major religions depend on information about God's reality from people that have been dead over one thousand to thousands of years? Then, there is the question of accuracy of the information we have today. Consider, we don't really know who wrote the Book of Genesis. Assume it was Moses. Is it logical to believe that an omnipotent and omniscient God would wait about 3,000 years – the most conservative estimate – then reveal to just one man the story of creation as well as the following years leading up to at least the time of Abraham? Nowhere in the Bible does it say that God gave Moses or anyone else this information. But where else could it have come from? Even Adam and Eve were not around to witness the first few days of creation. Surely, man's creative imagination filled in the gaps.

The point is that once certain religious teachings are accepted as unquestioned fact, such as, the Bible is the Word of God, even the most intellectual of humans can become illogical about some beliefs.

At least judged by scientific methods, many religious claims are illogical. However, the claim that God or a Supreme Being was the First Cause of all creation is logical (except claiming He created Himself). Science has no method to rule out this possibility and until it does, God as the original Creator remains a valid theory, we could say, "a religious fact."

Factually, science continually updates its truth with evolving new evidence, while religion prefers truth that was fixed thousands of years ago. The designation of being a holy man overcomes any scientific ignorance regardless of how far back in history an event or saying occurred. That is not to say that religion is not continually updated. It is done in the form of new sects and new interpretations, but rarely do religious people reject ancient truth from its accepted holy sources. The prime example is Christianity's 34,000 sects.

It seems that understanding God, or an invisible Spirit, based on logic alone is dependent on reasoning that is conditioned by one's previous experience.

Consider some unusual events that I have experienced in my over seventy years. Sometimes when I read or write I sit in a chair in the bedroom. Before I got new glasses I used to take my glasses off and throw them on the bed. I had done this many times, with the glasses always landing with the side pieces horizontal on the bedspread and the nose piece either up or down. One morning I had been thinking about the importance many believers place on signs or miracles. As I sat down to write and threw my glasses, they landed on the lens with the side pieces pointing vertically. In none of my previous throwing had my glasses ever landed this way. I amusingly questioned, "Is this a sign?" then shortly forgot about the incident.

Early one morning, about a month later, I was lying on the bed at our second home, again considering possibilities regarding signs or miracles. Suddenly one side of the room lit up with an arc or bow of light that went from the floor to across the ceiling and back down to the floor, it was like a rainbow, but consisted of only white light. I had slept in that bed probably a thousand times and had never seen this bow before. After investigating, I found that the blind had to be in a just-so position and when the sun rose to a certain point, it would produce this light effect for about ten minutes. This reminded me of the glasses anomaly, so I attempted to reproduce it. It took four tries before the glasses landed vertically. The most unusual thing about the two events was that they both occurred as I thought about religious signs. I have to wonder if a mind overstimulated by religious ideas, such as Mormonism's Joseph Smith likely experienced many times, would have interpreted a similar bow happening as a personal sign from God. Might he then fabricate a few extravagant details?

Now consider two stranger experiences I had. They are remarkable because I do not find a normal explanation for either one of them.

The first occurred in May 1996. About 5 AM one morning I was meditating on people I had once known that were then deceased. Suddenly my thought focused on the 1940s cowboy movie actor Lash Larue. He was quite vivid in my mind, dressed in his black outfit, with his long bullwhip in his hand. Later, as I contemplated this event, I could think of only one time in at least forty years that I had heard or thought of this cowboy from my childhood movie time. Some years earlier I had read a small article in a newspaper about Larue being in Jacksonville, Florida and dealing with, I believe, a substance abuse problem.

The really strange part occurred in the afternoon of that same day. I was filling my car at a Shell gas station in Conyers, Georgia. The pump was set on automatic, so I went over to a newspaper rack and began scanning the front page of a local paper in which I learned that Alfred Larue – movie name, Lash – had passed away the previous day.

The second mysterious event was even more bizarre, it was a dream I had in February of 2003. I was dreaming that I was talking to someone about nothing important when suddenly a boy from my high school days walked into the scene. I shall call him Roger. I said, "Roger, what are you doing here?" He replied, "I came to say good bye," then walked away. I awoke from my dream with a start. Around noon that day I got a call from my high school friend, Frances, with whom I have regular communication. She asked me to guess who died last night. I immediately said, "Roger Harper" – not his real name. "How did you find out so quickly?" she questioned, since she lived in the same general area as Roger, but I lived 450 miles away. Upon learning the source of my information, she was shocked.

As if this dream was not strange enough, it gets odder on considering the facts surrounding this incident. In 2003 it had been almost *fifty years* since my high school time – a time when I knew Roger only casually. We were never close friends, nor do I remember ever having more than a fifteen-minute encounter with him. Since high school I recall seeing him twice, both times at class reunions: at only one did we have a conversation. That conversation lasted about five minutes.

There is one more tid-bit to add concerning Roger. In the summer of 2007, I had a dinner date with some high school friends at a restaurant near our hometown. Just as I arrived, Frances called to say she and the others would be about forty-five minutes late. So I decided to kill the time riding around my hometown. As I turned onto a road that passed one of the town's cemeteries, I decided to see if I could find the grave of one of my best friends who was killed in a terrible auto accident in the 1950s.

Stopping on the road that divides the graves into two sections, I stepped out of the car with my feet being only inches from a marble slab. I glanced at the head stone. You probably guessed it – it was Roger's grave. Yet the grave incident can easily be chalked up to coincidence, as well as the glasses and the bow experiences.

But what is the rationalization to explain my mind's timing on Lash, or – especially – Roger? These events offer a real possibility that my brain received information from an outside source. Even if this source was my mind or consciousness, it could indicate communication with a universal consciousness in which case the brain simply received and transmitted the data to my physical awareness.

Does that indicate a logical connection between my strange experiences and God? Of course not! But these experiences certainly offer the potential that my mind is not a closed, self-generated loop that receives its information only from the physical senses. As to which is cause and which is effect regarding the brain-mind relationship, this relationship is not relevant to the fact that my awareness happens to have received information originating from another source.

Could that source be supernatural? Possibly! Revelation can be as valid a claim of logic as that of religion. The God of logic is no more definitive than the God of religion in that they both lead to the same place, that is mystery. Be it faith in logic or faith through religious belief, either is a guess that is assigned a higher value by calling it faith, that is not to say that religious belief is never logical.

As already stated, some religious beliefs are illogical, by logical, I mean reasonable. Therefore, illogical beliefs would mean unreasonable, or not based on known facts. The problem is many believers accept unscientific religious teachings as facts – no evidence to support those facts – then those believers use those unsupported facts to support their faith.

But even after accepting unsupported facts, once again, such as the Bible being the inerrant Word of God, further belief is sometimes unreasonable based on those facts. For example, Christianity, Judaism and Islam have faith that God is all-knowing, all powerful and in some manner, everywhere present. Does it seem reasonable for anyone to think Adam and Eve were the first couple and that they were created full grown with adult mental capabilities? Believers that say yes must use the justification that God can do anything.

If so, is it logical that that same God would be so vindictive about the first couple disobeying Him that he would take away their eternal life and sentence them to a life of hardship – not to mention that all future humanity would carry the burden of sin because of the first couple's disobedience, at least for thousands of years until God in His infinite mercy sent His only Son to endure a horrible death on earth. Because of His Son's sacrifice, God will forgive humans, that is, those humans that really believe and accept that God's Son died to wash away sin. This is essentially the Christian Gospel. How logical is it to believe that the smartest, most powerful, most loving and most merciful Power in the universe would order such a history? Also consider the logic of that same almighty Power ordering – as many believe – a future for sinners of eternal fiery burning.

Logically, would the Ultimate Authority in the universe create His alleged master work – a man and a woman – then take no responsibility for His creation disobeying Him one time, but rather punish the creation so severely? Some liberal Bible-defenders might argue that Genesis' creation story is not meant to be taken as literal history. The Catholic Church, for example, teaches that the creation as described in the Bible is mythic narrative, yet at the same time claims it to be actual history. Remember, today's definition of a myth does not necessarily mean that it is fiction, but rather it is something that cannot be proven by scientific facts.

Logically, I can find no justification for the most important historical event of all time to be revealed as a myth – particularly when so much else in the book that tells the story is taken literally, as written, to be an instruction for living during all time. For example, consider Catholicism's most important ceremony, that of the Eucharist which originated with the strange Bible verse that has Jesus saying to eat His flesh and drink His blood. Since Catholics cannot literally do that, the Church provides wine and wafers and teaches that they magically turn into Jesus' flesh and blood.

The illogical teaching about the first couple imposing sin on humanity really centers on theology. Christianity is stuck with the fact that Adam and Eve's disobedience must be a true history or else the Christian gospel of salvation is based on a false foundation.

I'll move away from this theological tangle and consider a simple fact. All Judeo-Christian-Islamic views about God never allow for the possibility that intelligent creatures may live on other worlds. What if intelligent species occupy other spheres in the universe? What if billions of other planets are populated by intelligent creatures? In the last decade science has confirmed the existence of planets in other solar systems and is discovering new ones all the time. How adaptable are the main religious views about the God of our planet to a universe swarming with life on other worlds? Since earth is much younger than many parts of the universe, this allows for the possibility that some alien creatures may have attained vastly superior intelligence to that of humankind.

I remember two religious figures separately being asked the question, "If intelligent beings occupy other worlds, do you think that the Christian gospel is their path to heaven?" Both essentially answered, "It is possible that human-like creatures live on other worlds. But I only know what God requires on our planet."

Plainly, the Christian gospel of salvation through faith in the blood of Jesus would not be very adaptable to heaven-seeking creatures on other planets, nor would Islam's path of Mohammed and the Koran. Of course, Christian and Islamic apologists might see this as proof that there are no human-like creatures on other planets.

Consider that Buddhism's doctrine of impermanence applies to everything, not just the soul. Nothing has permanent identity. Everything we see is in a continual state of change. There appears to be no reason this concept could not be applied to everything in the universe. Also, Hinduism's one absolute of all creation being the only reality, could fit the philosophy of creatures on one world or on a trillion worlds – that is, of course, to beings who found such a teaching acceptable.

Interestingly, the more mystical religions of Buddhism and Hinduism appear to have a universal application while earth's two largest religions seem limited to our planet. Notwithstanding that the flexibility of interpretation, especially as practiced by many followers of Hinduism, appears to favor limiting religious understanding to a very localized geography. This is found in the numerous examples of villages, towns or regions having their own special deity to whom is directed devotion.

Ponder the previously-mentioned teachings of Judaism that Jesus taught are the two greatest commandments: to love God and to love your neighbor. This may be the best instruction from any of our religious sources that can find application anywhere in the universe. If every intelligent creature in the universe envisioned a God of love and reflected that ideal in love of his neighbor by establishing the golden rule as the prime mandate, there would be no need for any complex theology.

A Supreme Being called God or other names may be more favorable to logic as the First Cause of creation than that of unguided nature. Why? Because something – God – creates something else. Nature would have its beginning in nothingness. But is it not just as fair to say that natural laws have eternally existed as it is to claim that God always has been? Yes, but with an unguided nature it seems more problematic that life would ever originate and ultimately produce mind and intelligence, whereas God was a pre-existent pattern of life, mind and intelligence. The bottom line – God appears to trump unguided nature as the more logical choice for being the First Cause of creation.

What about the hereafter? Is that a logical belief? I say yes, but not along the lines of religious teachings that have dead, physical bodies returning to life in heaven or anywhere else. Mind or consciousness seems to be energy that transports and processes information. When the brain is included as part of this system, science assures us that energy in the form of electrical impulses is essential to transmitting brain-mind data.

Science also tells us that energy is never destroyed: it may be transformed from one state to another, including that of matter; however, energy never ceases to be. The question, then, becomes what form does the mind's energy take at physical death of body and brain, which are known to decay into oblivion. Is it also the mind's fate to decay into a state that no longer relates to awareness; or does consciousness survive in a new state of being?

Consider that science can tell us how a memory survives in the brain as a structure composed of groups of nerve cells that were a part of a particular experience. Future brain activity may retrieve information from these memory patterns somewhat like a computer does. But computers store and retrieve the same data that was inputted. The brain's storage of an event is determined by the way a person thinks. Two people may experience the same event, yet their stored memory may be considerably different. And the retrieval of a memory in our brain may be obscured by how we think – such as thoughts of an emotional nature. Of course, time may distort or discard our memories.

In any case, memory is being explained in physical terms, based mainly on data provided by functional MRI that maps areas of brain function. Some people accept this kind of information as an explanation of human consciousness. Both Gary Schwartz and Deepak Chopra have previously told us that no one knows how consciousness originates in our brain. This means the possibility exists that the brain may function only as a receiver-transmitter that is analogous to a TV set. However, a TV has no ability to experience, whereas the brain processes an experience by arranging nerve cells into a pattern or an imprint that may reproduce the memory of a particular experience – if called on to do so by one's consciousness. In this case, the consciousness would be the equivalent of a broadcasting station that transmits a program to the brain. However, unlike a TV set that retrieves the same program it received, the brain adjusts its reception by mixing current data with all its stored past experience. The result is that each individual human brain might produce a unique interpretation of the data that reaches each person's awareness. Thus, any explanation concerning the operation of memory in our brain does nothing to hinder the possibility that consciousness may reside in a non-physical state that could function without need of a particularly physical body or brain. Therefore, logic seems to support the possibility of awareness surviving physical death, at least, *my* logic says it is reasonable to believe in God and also in a hereafter, although neither is necessarily dependent on the other.

God's existence does not guarantee any type of survival for human consciousness. And if unguided nature actually produced life as well as indestructible energy, why could not that same nature support the continuation of consciousness in the afterlife?

All this may reflect my natural ignorance, but as repeatedly stated, science cannot presently rule out God's existence, nor the possibility of one's consciousness continuing in a next life. Of course, not being able to rule out, does not mean proof of anything. Thus, present science must allow for the possibility of God as well as a hereafter, although a well-respected scientist has subtitled his very informative book, *How Science Shows that God Does not Exist.*

This, will be explored in the next chapter.

11 UNGUIDED NATURE

If there is no God or a Supreme Intelligence that originates and maintains the universe, then that leaves us with only one other logical choice to be the most powerful force ever imagined. This force is unguided nature.

Victor J. Stenger is emeritus professor of physics and astronomy at the University of Hawaii and adjunct professor of philosophy at the University of Colorado. He is also the author of many articles and books. His *God the Failed Hypothesis* plainly accepts unguided nature as the first cause and maintainer of the universe.

Professor Stenger does not agree with his colleagues who think that science should limit its study to natural phenomena. Like Richard Dawkins, he posits that if God is an active cause in the universe, then science should be able to show some evidential effects of God in the natural world. Using solid, observable science in his search, Stenger finds observations from cosmology, physics, quantum mechanics and other things to "look just as they can be expected to look if there is no God."

On the jacket cover of Stenger's book, Richard Dawkins says "I learned an enormous amount from this splendid book!" In his book *The God Delusion*, Dawkins – relying on his expertise in biology and other observations – arrives at the same conclusion as Stenger, namely, that the universe looks as it should, without any need for God.

Stenger's book makes a strong case for the atheistic position. He supports his conclusions with detailed evidence. He covers a range of subjects. On page 23 he addresses an issue that relates to my puzzling experiences concerning Lash and Roger. Stenger cites examples of dreams that came true that might suggest the mind's ability to exceed known physical capabilities. He explains this as "a strong selection process taking place whereby all the millions of dreams that do not come true are simply ignored." Without a better explanation to be ruled out, "the reported dream came true by chance selection out of many" dreams that did not come true.

In my examples I don't think chance selection is the answer. Nor is chance selection specific to either event. Roger's visit occurred in a dream, while thoughts of Lash came during meditation. My dream about Roger made no suggestion that he was either dead or dying, that is, unless Roger's telling that he had come to say goodbye was interpreted to mean he would soon be dead or was already deceased. I believe the better explanation is that my consciousness did not originate this information; rather, it received it from another source and until science can explain consciousness in physical terms that falsify my view, an outside source is the more satisfactory answer to me. That is not to say that an outside source must be supernatural. It could be that Roger's brain or consciousness in some way communicated with me by a process that science has yet to discover.

If unguided nature is the absolute driving force of all creation, then the possibility exists to explain everything in physical terms. Said another way, the concept is that everything can be explained naturally. Any gaps in present knowledge will gradually be overcome as science evolves. Should humankind survive a thousand or a million years from now, I have to wonder how much present ignorance will be overcome. Or, at some future time, will humankind self-destruct and regress to more primitive ways, or perhaps even disappear? An unguided nature has no preference for either outcome.

Unguided nature, seen as the first cause, answers some of our greatest questions this way:

> Is there a Creator that humankind knows as God? No.

Is there any survival of human consciousness after physical death? Possibly.

Where did the universe come from? Nowhere.

What is the purpose of life? Nothing.

Why am I here? This evolved through a random process governed by mutations that were produced by natural selection.

Is it logical or reasonable to believe that the first cause of creation was nothing? The vast majority of humanity would quickly answer NO. But on page 129 of Stenger's book, a subchapter begins that is entitled, *Where Do the Laws of Physics Come From?* In it, Stenger frankly admits that his views on the subject are not recognized by a consensus of physicists – while at the same time he insists that his science is well established and conventional. He scientifically supports his conclusion that the laws of physics came from "nothing." Stenger closes this subchapter by arguing that he has provided a plausible natural possibility for a gap in scientific knowledge concerning the origin of physical law. He also asserts that any believer who thinks that God originates that law, that same believer has the burden of proof to show that Stenger is wrong.

In his next subchapter that starts on page 132, Stenger stresses that current physics and cosmology support that "something is more natural than nothing." Further, he claims that God would not be required for the natural "transition of nothing-to-something." Surprisingly, he concludes that an empty universe rather than a full one would require the work of an agent like God in order to maintain a "state of nothingness."

Since Stenger grounds his arguments in science, other scientists can now validate or falsify his hypothesis. The God that Victor Stenger finds that does not exist is the

One worshipped by most Jews, Christians and Muslims – a considerable portion of the world's population, a population that does not agree on a plethora of significant issues. On page 231, he lists eleven hypothetical observations that, if science could confirm even one, "would force even the most dogmatic skeptic to reconsider his atheism." But so far, Stenger finds no such confirmation.

There is a saying that approximates: if ten atheists were thrown overboard in the middle of an ocean, some of them would appeal to God to save themselves. It is somewhat scary to think of unguided nature as the ultimate force in the universe – a force totally detached from all outcomes. This would mean that it did not matter whether those thrown overboard either survived or perished. The only difference in this view and that of Deepak Chopra's depiction of Brahman is that Brahman imagines everything, which would require some type of intelligence, while unguided nature is simply a blind and deaf cause that creates when random chance presents the opportunity for a trial and error process to begin.

Since unguided nature requires no purpose to life, it also has no objection to intelligent beings choosing to give a purpose to life – even if it is the choice to serve a God that is the product of human imagination.

With the help of Stenger's science, perhaps we could rewrite Genesis' creation story: in the beginning there was nothing, but nothing was an unnatural state since there exists no agent to maintain a state of nothingness. Suddenly, with an enormous Big Bang, nothing made the transition of becoming something. Now that we have something to work with, we can look to present-day science to finish the story. Something, probably consisting of infinitely small, vibrating strings, began to produce an abundance of energy and matter. By means of collision and explosion, the laws of physics came into being and began to set up boundaries and exercise controls on the chaos. Organization and order began to mold a pattern for a predictable universe of material matter and energy, although most matter and most energy remains invisible.

All this "something" continues to evolve through a random process of trial and error and within the limitations of the laws of physics. In order to fill the empty void, more and more something evolved into stars, planets, galaxies as well as visible and invisible energy and matter. Today we know that the universe is an expanding one that is now at least 13.75 billion years old and that very recently – in real time – it produced us human beings. Over the last century, the age of the universe has been updated several times. Presently, its age is largely determined by measuring the length of time it takes light to reach us. Scientific instruments and methods reveal that light from the farthest observable stars took almost 14 billion years to travel to the earth. Considering that light travels at 186,300 or so miles per second – or over 670 million miles per hour – the galaxy that houses those stars at the observable boundary of the universe is almost unbelievably far away. In fact, most of its stars that we see today have long ago exploded, thereby producing material that created new stars, new planets and other cosmic energy-matter. Other of its stars have imploded into black holes.

Thus, what we now see of stars is what they looked like in the past. If their light took a thousand or billions of years to reach the earth, then our information about them is that many years out of date. Consider, since the universe is an expanding one, all the while light has been traveling to us from distant galaxies, those same galaxies have been traveling away from us at ever-increasing speed. In fact, the normal impression that light from the oldest galaxy that took 13 billion years to get here is that that galaxy may now be twice that far distant is wrong. The truth is that it is even farther away. On page 156 of his book, Stenger says that the farthest observable galaxy, known as ABELL, is now about 40 billion light-years away. It is hard for us to conceptualize this astronomical distance, just like it is hard to conceptualize the speed of light.

So why does science generally accept the accuracy of the universe's age since it includes outdated data? Because it correlates and confirms the scientifically acceptable model of the Big Bang origin of our universe: that all the energy-matter – and some say space itself – was originally compressed into an area smaller than an atom. For debatable reasons, on the first instant of creation, all that pent-up, infinitely small bundle of energy-matter suddenly exploded. In the first tiny fraction of a second of that now famous Big Bang, the particles of created energy-matter expanded in all directions at a speed much faster than that of light. As those particles began to cool, and the laws of physics began to exercise control, no particle – within a localized region of space-time – could exceed the universe's speed limit that was restricted to the speed of light.

So when we say the age of the universe is 13.75 billion years, it also means that it is the length of time since the Big Bang. But I just said the universe had a speed limit on matter equal to the speed of light. Then how could we observe the galaxy ABELL that Victor Stenger said is some 40 billion light-years distant?

To compound this question, Wikipedia's article on the universe states that the diameter of the observable universe is at least 93 billion light-years. How can that be? Apply some basic math to the fact that matter can travel no faster than the speed of light and that the farthest matter's light took 13.75 billion years to get here. The matter that took the opposite direction should not have been able to travel more than the distance of an additional 13.75 billion light-years. Hence, the farthest it should now be from us is no more than 27.5 billion light years. But Stenger says that it is about half again farther away and Wikipedia tells us the universe is observed to be a minimum of 93 billion light-years across. We must look to the work of possibly the greatest scientific mind of all time for an answer to this seeming paradox. Albert Einstein's special theory of relativity states that matter cannot travel at a speed greater than that of light within a localized region of space-time – such as within a galaxy. But Einstein's general theory of relativity says that space can stretch or expand with no known limit on its speed. Thus, space between galaxies can expand faster than the speed of light. So this super speed expansion of space allows scientists to observe the light and calculate the distance of a galaxy that is now much farther than 27.5 billion light-years away.

Current observations show space between galaxies is increasing speed due to dark energy – one of science's great mysteries. In fact, it appears that ordinary matter makes up only 4 percent of the universe. Dark energy accounts for 73 percent; the remaining 23 percent is classed as cold dark matter. This means that 96 percent of the matter and energy in the universe is not directly observable. Thus, their properties remain mostly unknown. Why this science lesson from an author, I, who is not really qualified to give one? The main point is to show the incredible kind of information that science has revealed about the workings of the universe without any need for a God as taught by organized religion: rather, science can attribute the workings of the universe to unguided nature!

Concurrent with training and experience with scientific methods, it is easy to understand how claims about the God of Abraham and many Christian theological teachings began to turn the scientific-minded toward agnosticism or atheism.

However, I have to side with the crowd that disagrees with professors Stenger and Dawkins, both of whom believe that "science shows that God does not exist" and that unguided nature is necessarily the ultimate creator of the universe. At the same time I can agree with these prominent scientists that the Judeo-Christian-Islamic God as popularly portrayed possibly does not exist. Rather, humankind's favorite version of God may be a product of human imagination and idealistic creativity.

The one thing we can be certain of is that we "are here." Yet uncertainty abounds about who or what was the initial cause of our being here, or, for that matter, the uncertainty of the identity of the first cause of anything at all being here.

While it is understandable why the scientific-minded tend to reject popular religious views about God, science itself is producing information that gives support to a more mysterious theory of creation than anything the world's religious texts have revealed. A good example is the invisible and essentially unknown 96 percent of the universe. Although Stenger's book on page 157 says that this mass "is not even of the type of matter associated with life."

So much of human communication depends on definitions attached to words. If scientists simply chose a name, such as "God stuff," instead of dark energy and cold dark matter, then science could accept God as a reality. Of course, science's God would be dramatically different from that of humanity's present understanding of the word God. Rather than get bogged down in fixed creeds and fixed teachings, as most of organized religion has done, science will reveal ever-new facts about the mysteries of the universe; and just as in the past and present, scientists will believe science is on the verge of explaining everything, only to discover the appearance of a new, more complex mystery.

Nature could be the single most powerful force in the universe. But it seems to include way too much mystery to conclude that it is unguided.

Present-day science has revealed adequate information to question or rule out much in the way of religious teachings. Perhaps at some future time science will confirm some natural intelligence at work in the cosmos that would trump unguided nature. Of course, if it is ever discovered that nature has been guided by Intelligence, humankind will then have proof of God. But it will not be proof of the God that most of the world's organized religions have depicted. Curiously, Hinduism's core concept of an all-encompassing, absolute of creation might turn out to be humankind's best idea of the reality of God, even though that idea has been blurred by elements of impersonality or personality.

Another interesting point, should unguided nature win out as the universe's ultimate power, it does not necessarily follow that there is no hereafter for human consciousness, as previously suggested: whatever entity is the first cause or maintainer of the universe that we observe today, based on past performance, surely that thing has the ability to support the continuation of consciousness in a future life or state.

12 PERSONAL EXPERIENCE

This book began with a pair of adolescent minds, stimulated by a movie, imagining trees becoming monsters. Childhood and teenage imagination can produce some very strange concepts. As a child, I remember that stories about haunted houses or spooky places took on a vivid reality in my mind.

As a teenager of driving age, on hearing of a local scary location, I endeavored to check it out. Abandoned, isolated houses commonly got the reputation of being haunted. Several times, friends and I made nighttime visits to a so-called haunted house. Seldom did we ever get inside before one of us claimed to see something eerie and we all scrambled back to the car and took off.

One place of interest was located on a country road, beside a fence that blocked access to a small pond. If you parked there and kept quiet, within a few minutes you were supposed to hear the heavy footsteps of something walking around the pond. Of course, this had to be done at night; during daylight hours nothing weird occurred. Friends and I made many visits to this haunted place and at one time or the other, every one of us heard those footsteps.

One day, while I was talking about the footsteps with an older man, he gave me some new information. He told me to go, late at night, to the railroad tracks that crossed this road near the footsteps' location and stop on the tracks. If I looked down the tracks, soon I would see a distant form moving towards me; supposedly, this was the ghost of a woman that had been killed on these tracks. On two occasions I parked at the appropriate place with a car-load of other fellows. Although some of my companions claimed to have seen something, I myself saw only vacant railroad tracks.

Some weeks later I again had a conversation with the man who had told me about the railroad ghost. I advised him about the results of my attempted sightings. His reply was that the ghost made its best appearances around midnight. As I had lived most of my life in this small town, with less than 10,000 people in the entire county, and the fact that this man, only recently, was the first person to ever mention this ghost story, I began to suspect he had made it up. Although my visits to the railroad track took place before 9 PM, his story just didn't add up. Soon, the legend of the woman on the tracks slipped from my mind.

Months later, I was driving home alone after taking my friend Johnny to his home several miles into the country. The time was about midnight. I soon realized that I was only about a mile away from the supposed haunted railroad track. Shortly, I stopped on that very track. Furtively, I glanced around the desolate place, being careful to keep the motor running and the doors locked. I began to look for the woman. Being alone generated a sense of fear and uneasiness that was not present with a car full of other boys. After spending a few uncomfortable minutes, I was sure a figure was coming down the tracks toward me. As the apparition moved closer, a disabling sense of fear began to paralyze me. It rooted me to the spot. Even as I sensed the element of danger, I was increasingly less able to do anything about it. A very tall, dark form seemed to be floating in the air and was rapidly approaching. Then, as if I were moving in slow motion, I slammed the clutch pedal to the floor, put my old Plymouth in gear and speedily made my exit – all the while pondering what I had just experienced.

Then, as a teenager, and now as an older adult, I have always been curious about claims of the supernatural. But my mind has approached these claims with an inherent skepticism.

I believe these youthful ghost stories reveal much insight into religion, reality and even discourse on the hereafter. For instance, personal experience has taught me that one can pick a location on any lonely road in America and then create a story about being there late at night, and by staying very still and quiet, eventually footsteps or other supposed sounds can be heard. This is most effective with individuals who are not familiar with the location.

As to the apparition I saw on the railroad tracks years ago, after careful thought and further investigation, I now believe the truth is quite simple. On the night of my sighting there was a full moon that allowed good vision down the tracks. It was also rather windy. What I saw was not a ghost, but rather the shadows of the branches from the many trees that paralleled the railroad. As the wind blew the tree limbs, their shadows gave the illusion of something moving down the railroad tracks. The "footsteps" by the pond easily translate to the awareness of one's own heart pounding; the phenomenon may also be reported as "distant marching" or "distant drumming." Thus, I conclude that with proper investigation, so many claims of reported miracles made by religious sources can be exposed as mere natural occurrences or deceit.

The power of suggestion is another potent force in shaping belief. Had it never been known to me that a ghost could be seen, I probably would have experienced nothing out of the ordinary by looking down the tracks that night. The same holds true for the suggestion that footsteps can be heard at a particular isolated place.

Over the years, from the early 1960s and into the 1990s, there were numerous reports of individual encounters with or abductions by aliens that were associated with UFO events. Usually under hypnosis, the victims vividly described similar incidents. Then, experts began to accept that it was the unintended suggestions posed by the hypnotist's questions that unfolded in the victim's account of their believed encounter. Reports of UFO sightings continue, but the report of aliens visiting humans has become a rare event.

The word "suggest" has been defined by Webster as to mention, introduce or propose (an idea, plan, person, or etc.)

for consideration, possible action or some purpose or use. Suggestions can be conveyed orally or by other means – by books, by other printed material (electronic means, etc.). Fact, fiction, falsehood, truth, theory and partial knowledge may all take root in suggestion. Now consider that most religious authority is rooted in humans claiming communication with the divine and this has mainly occurred on a one-on-one basis. In other words, there were no witnesses to these monumental events. Abraham, Moses and the prophets, in the Old Testament; John the Baptist, Paul, Saint John and Jesus in the New Testament; Mohammed in the Muslim religion; and, in later times Mormonism's Joseph Smith. In modern times, evangelists such as the late Oral Roberts, all claimed direct communication from God or a divine representative.

Of course, throughout history as well as currently, a great number of people have been reported to have received direct revelation from God. But it is only the claims that are accepted by a group of followers that form the foundation for a religion or religious authority. Why are some suggested revelations accepted and other rejected? Why, for example, did early Christians accept Judaism's established prophets and scriptures while most Jews rejected Jesus and New Testament writings as divine authority? Then, in turn, hundreds of years later, Islam accepted Jewish and Christian prophets and scriptures – at least, those that did not conflict with the teachings of Mohammed and the Koran, while Jews and Christians alike rejected the authority of both Mohammed and the Koran.

The bulk of religious teaching in the world today centers on the story of Abraham. It incorporates the beginning of humankind in the Adam and Eve drama, which is popularly accepted as occurring about 2,000 years before Abraham's time. The Bible's version of these two great milestones in human history bridges this span of time by attributing lifespan of hundreds of years to certain individuals. Methuselah, at 969 years, lived the longest time. While today's reality sees such a lengthy lifetime as impossible, Bible literalists justify the time with sayings like, "Back then there were very few germs or other micro-organisms that could cause disease and thus people could live hundreds of years."

Perhaps the author of such long lives used a different yardstick in measuring years as compared to today. In fact, 969 months would be just over 80 years, which in reality was a long lifespan in ancient time. Of course, if an ancient biblical year was only the equivalent of today's month, the span of time between Adam and Abraham would be less than 170 of today's years. Another reasonable explanation could be that Methuselah, together with his long-lived relatives, was simply a product of the writer's imagination. However, my purpose here is not to again explore problems related to a literal Bible's relation to reality, rather to explore the concept of suggestion at work in the personal experience of religious folks.

Around 2500 years ago Jewish scholars had reduced their scriptures to writing. The body of facts suggested by their text is the major underpinning for the majority of religious belief in our time. Factually, the Hebrews established this underpinning with the God of Abraham as expressed by the Old Testament! Oddly, they never actively sought converts to their religion. But, later, Christianity – and still later, Islam – made conversion of the masses a major element of their teachings. Thus, today both Christianity and Islam have more than 100 times as many adherents as Judaism. Of note, Islam's existence of about 1400 years is 70 percent of Christianity's time-span. Interestingly, Islam is approaching 70 percent as many followers as Christianity. This appears to indicate that aggressive missionary effort on behalf of a religion will produce more new members than the content of that religion's message.

This brings to mind a conversation I had with a previously not very dedicated Christian. He had recently joined and had become a strong supporter of an evangelical church that through aggressive proselytizing had acquired one of the largest congregations in the United States. I had attended three services at this church after repeated invitations from my friend. A few days after the third service I was questioning this friend about the truth's relation to some of the instructions that the head pastor had given in his sermons. The pastor was very literally-Bible-minded. My friend defended the pastor's sermons by saying "Would God have let this church grow into a congregation of many thousands of members if the preacher was not teaching the truth?" I replied, "Based on your logic, you cannot question the truth of Islam, for example, since it has over one billion followers." This event occurred about five years ago and since then I've had no more invitations to his church. Moreover, since then he even avoids any religious discussion around me.

The one element common to all spiritual faiths is that it is developed through personal experience. The seeds that grow into spiritual faith are mostly planted by the suggestions of extant religious teachings. Interpretations of the Old Testament developed the seeds that sprouted into the New Testament. The Old and New Testaments produced interpretations that cultivated the field that grew the Koran.

Of course, without great spiritual teachers such as Jesus, Moses and Mohammed, their related sayings could never have been turned into holy texts by their followers. Due to the lack of non-religious historical confirmation, some argue that Moses was probably a composite creation for teaching purposes, rather than an actual man. There are even those who question not only the divinity, but the human existence of Jesus as a historical figure. That is because there are so few known, brief, non-religious references to a man named Jesus Who was put to death by the Romans around 30 CE. There is, however, no doubt that the existence of Mohammed was an historical fact.

In any case, the teachings of rabbis, priests and preachers of today derive their authority from the Bible and that of imams, from the Koran; and it is the commentary derived from these texts, and established legal codes from these texts that produce the suggestions that influence the personal experience of believers. In the case of Catholicism, church tradition is stated to be of equal authority as the Bible; and, as Catholicism rightly claims, it was church tradition that decided on the content of the Christian Bible. Of course, there are smaller sects of Christianity that equate this authority of their own special texts or traditions to that of the Bible. For example, Mormonism has the *Book of Mormon, Doctrine and Covenants*, and the *Pearl of Great Price*. Most Mormons view these texts as adherents of other denominations and other religious people view their own special text, that is, as extensions of their sacred writings.

In any case, the personal experience of each new generation with the established experience of past generations develops the suggestions that lead to the belief that continually produces the religious faith of individuals in each age.

What, then, caused the great bifurcation of Judaism, Christianity and Islam, since each claims its foundation as the God of Abraham? I posit it is that ever-present human tendency to exert power and control over the structure of other people's faith.

A story from my own experience illustrates this possibility. My first wife-to-be was a dedicated, observing Catholic and naturally wanted to be married by a priest. As my parents came from very different religious backgrounds, I had grown up with about equal exposure to Jewish and Southern Baptist religious teachings. By the time I considered marriage, I had no preference for any particular religion and knew practically nothing about Catholicism. On meeting with a priest to make service arrangements, I was informed that since I was not Catholic, there were conditions I must agree to in order to have a Catholic wedding. It was preferable to the church that I become Catholic, but it was not absolutely mandatory. Instead, I could undergo a course of study supervised by a priest and I must agree that any children of our marriage must be raised Catholic.

I thought it might be interesting to learn about Catholicism; and, since her faith was so important to my fiancée, I had no objection to children being trained in her church. Soon I began reading the book given me by the priest. Originally, I was impressed: both the logic of its content and the explanations of theological truths were well connected. Then, I found a statement that was very objectionable to my thinking. This happened so many years ago that I don't recall what it said. But I do remember my next meeting with the priest when I voiced my objection. He essentially said, "The source of that statement is church tradition. No one questions tradition." My study of Catholicism on the church's terms ended right there. My feeling was that the church was more concerned about its power to control its parishioners' thinking than it was to search for truth.

The priest was still willing to marry us if I would sign papers guaranteeing any children we had would be raised Catholic. I said I would agree to Catholic-reared children, but found it unacceptable to sign legal documents to that effect. What difference would putting it in writing make? The priest admitted the church would not resort to any legal action. Anyway, we were married by a justice of the peace and our two children were raised Catholic by my wife with no interference from me.

Just how does my marriage story relate to the three religions of Abraham choosing such different paths to knowing the same one God? Individual personal experience with suggestions from religious sources mold belief that is strongly accepted as the religious faith of a particular person. Once faith is institutionalized, that very organization limits flexibility and strictly binds its followers, thus the distinction between faith in God and faith in a particular religious organization becomes blurred. If the individual's faith in God is at odds with an institution's system of faith, then that person has several choices:

Conform to the organization's system and ignore the areas of disagreement. To a large degree, this is expressed by people who actively participate in a particular denomination mainly as a tradition or as for social purposes, while the search for truth is of little concern. They appear religious, but are spiritually lazy.

Associate with a more agreeable institution.

Abandon institutionalized religion – similar to what many so-called new-agers have done.

Create an alternate religious system that may evolve into a new institution. This is seen in the different paths taken by the three major Abrahamic religions.

Abandon faith in God for faith in the physical world. This is seen partially in the choice of agnosticism and is fully expressed in the acceptance of atheism.

Make no commitment to any particular religion's system, but search for truth wherever it may appear. My own personal experience beckons in this direction and, like science's truth, my truth is always subject to change as new knowledge is received.

How did power and control affect the separation and conflict between the three religions of Abraham? Once Judaism had evolved to the status of an institution, a few wealthy Jews, elders and priests exercised firm power and control over the thinking and action of the Hebrew people. Generally, God was presented and should be approached not as God of the individual, but God of the group – the entire Hebrew population. Appropriate behavior of the individual was dictated by the religious leaders and any violation of their firm mandates could result in a death penalty for the offender.

There was no separation of civil and religious rules. God was seen as the giver of all law, thus an individual who broke God's law could bring punishment on the entire Hebrew community. Military defeat, captivity, disease and all sorts of hardship could be explained as God's retribution for the sins and iniquities of the people of Israel – the very ones who were said to be so precious to the Lord.

The Jews were often under the rule of stronger nations. Jewish authorities probably created the idea of "a chosen people" teaching as an effort to elevate the pride of a despondent people and give them a special sense of purpose.

During Jesus' time the Romans ruled over the Jews, but if no Roman laws were broken, the Jewish authorities could enforce their own laws on their own people. Going back to the death of King Solomon, the Jews had anticipated a new king of the order of David who would restore "the chosen people" to their former greatness by overcoming the enemy and freeing them of foreign rule.

In this setting, the first century, a Jew named Jesus chose twelve other Jews to assist Him in His public ministry. The Jewish scriptures were the teaching text utilized by Jesus. But He portrayed God in a personal relationship with the individual, as opposed to the existing concept of God of the Hebrew nation.

Jesus did not restrict His message to "a chosen people," but rather taught that the God of the Jews was the God of all people. This teaching, as well as other new sayings, was mixed with the Jewish scriptures. The ministry of Jesus began to attract many new followers – both Jews and Gentiles – and, of course, this became a serious threat to the power and control of the Jewish officials whose institutionalized inflexibility interpreted these new teachings as heresy. The resultant death of Jesus did not terminate this threat to Jewish authority. Instead, it allowed disciples of Jesus to passionately elevate

Jesus to the status of being the only Son of God. The Messiah, or King, the Jews expected was converted by Christian theologians from a military King David to a spiritual King Jesus Who bestows rewards in the hereafter to His followers. Although there is debate to this day, generally, Christianity sees belief as more important than acts or works in order to secure the rewards of Jesus' spiritual Kingdom.

I should clarify that by Jesus' time, Jewish beliefs about a Messiah-King (the Anointed One) to restore Israel's former greatness to that experienced under David was not fixed among Jews. But it appeared to be the dominant belief. Another long-running Jewish belief was that a future Messiah would not be limited to the nation of Israel, rather would come as a savior to the entire world. This would be a world that would become a new idealized earth of peace and harmony, where "the beasts from the wild will be led by a child."

This long-running belief about a future Messiah for the entire world was adopted and refined by Christians who taught that those who accepted and believed the gospel would get a heavenly reward. And it was this, spiritual kingdom of Christianity that would influence future Jewish ideas concerning the Messiah in that He would be of a more spiritual nature. In fact, some elements of Judaism accept that the Messiah is analogous to reaching a higher state of consciousness; while other Jews have discarded the idea of the long-overdue Messiah as important to their beliefs.

The easier Christian way of just believing combined with aggressive proselytizing and eventually the granting of civil power from Rome. Soon, this turned Christianity into not only the largest religion of the God of Abraham, but also later into the world's largest religion. And as Christianity rapidly grew, the rather simple message of Paul, "To believe in the Lord Jesus Christ and be saved" turned into a complex theological tangle that maintained that basic message at its core.

However, what became so confusing was just what is to be believed about Jesus? That His Mother was a virgin? That He is the one and only Son of God? That He performed miracles, including raising the dead? That He Himself returned from death? That He came to earth to redeem humankind from sin? That as witnesses watched, He bodily ascended to heaven? That He will return to earth and the saved will zoom up to the sky to meet Him? Just to relate a few problematic sayings. Too much theological baggage converted the religion *of* Jesus into a religion *about* Jesus. Just what *was* the religion of Jesus? I believe He spelled it out quite plainly in His instruction of the two greatest commandments: to love God and to love your neighbor.

Of course, the teachings of Paul and others who credited their work as Paul's were major contributors to this complexity.

By Mohammed's time, Judaism and Christianity had long since branched into two distinct religions and although Christianity was gathering vastly more adherents than Judaism, the Jews usually maintained a policy of welcoming new members into their community only at the request of an interested party. Thus, while Christianity began as a new sect within Judaism, Islam started as a new religion that worshiped the Abrahamic God and accepted many of the then-established teachings about Him.

Quoting from page 1010 of *The Urantia Book*, "In the sixth century after Christ Mohammed founded a religion which was superior to many of the creeds of his time. His was a protest against the social demands of the faiths of foreigners and against the incoherence of the religious life of his own people." The concept of foreigners, I believe, mainly addresses the presence of Christians and Jews of that day. Page 67 of the same source confirms that "Mohammedanism provides deliverance from the rigorous moral standards of Judaism and Christianity."

Thus, by the seventh century CE, the religion of Abraham had become two distinct religions of which Mohammed found neither acceptable. During the pre-Christian era, the great Hebrew King David had united the scattered nomadic tribes of his people into a single strong nation. But while David embraced the existing teachings of Judaism, Mohammed, who was also a military and civil ruler that united a scattered people, developed a still different path to the God of Abraham than that of either Judaism or Christianity. The practical application of his way, constituting the third path to the God of Abraham, is known as the five pillars of Islam. These are listed as:

A declaration of faith, in which one says, "There is no god but Allah and Mohammed is the messenger of God."

Prayer. Muslims pray five times during the day, starting at daybreak and ending in the evening.

Zakat or tithing, meaning "purification." The requirement to make an annual contribution of 2.5 percent of one's total net assets (not just one's income) for support of the poor.

Ramadan. Each year during the month of *Ramadan*, healthy Muslims must fast from dawn to sunset.

Pilgrimage *(hajj)*. Every adult Muslim who is physically and financially able is required to make a journey from his home to Mecca, Saudi Arabia at least once during his lifetime.

All three of the Abrahamic religions claim direct revelation and guidance from divinity. No one can say with certainty which claims are true or which claims are false. Each individual must determine that based on his or her own personal experience. Perhaps the best way to evaluate any religion is to observe how the majority of its adherents live their life in relation to the rest of humanity.

My personal observation and experience with the many suggestions offered by the various views of lay believers and scholars about the monotheistic God of Abraham finds considerable conflict within all three religions' teachings. However, it does seem that the essence of the intent of the religions of Jesus, Moses and Mohammed is a common goal to love God and to treat other humans fairly. Certainly the Old Testament, the New Testament and the Koran each have passages that can be used to dispute that goal; but they also contain many more passages within these sources that can support that goal.

Thus far, a consistent message of this book is that every religion or sect that has been explored in any detail offers a wealth of confusion. How an individual human mind interprets one's relation or non-relation with God is overwhelmingly the result of personal religious experience. And this experience can produce some very different views as regards holy text.

I believe that Deepak Chopra's book the *Third Jesus* is a great example of this difference. Since his childhood Chopra has been firmly grounded in the mystical and complex belief of Hinduism. Yet he artfully blends his training and knowledge of science into his spirituality. He applies this mindset to an interpretation of Jesus and the New Testament experience, thereby expressing terms that are completely at odds with popular Christian teachings about faith. Chopra portrays a Jesus Who "taught His followers how to reach God-consciousness." For example, on page 36, Chopra posits the Christian goal to enter God's Kingdom, which Christian believers equate to a hereafter in heaven; whereas Chopra finds much evidence in the Gospels that God's Kingdom is achieved in reaching a higher level of consciousness. In support of his position he gives new views to much of the New Testament. On page 20 Chopra explained that "consciousness is universal, and if there is such a thing as God consciousness, no one can be excluded from it." He also points out that no one can lay exclusive claim, either. The lesson here is that religious institutions can claim to teach the one and only truth, but only the believer's consciousness can accept it as unquestioned faith.

Put another way, faith is the product of personal religious experience. If that experience evolves from contact mainly with the suggestions of a particular religious source, be it Judaism or Christianity or Islam or another source – even study of the material world – then one's belief about God tends to accept the tenets of his exposure, thus there should be little mystery in how the God of Abraham can be understood by three separate faiths.

The only way a human mind can ever obtain real faith in God is by the technique of personal religious experience. This remains true even if most of that experience is filtered through the many erroneous teachings of man-made religious institutions. It is still possible for a human consciousness to develop true faith. And, of course, the atheist rejects the reality of God because he or she finds no satisfactory way to express God in material terms.

As to the hereafter, the closest thing to proof that the human mind can experience can be found in a living faith. But even the strongest faith may explore the potentials inherent in the next life. Is the hereafter a place equivalent to a new-idealized earth for the good folks and a place of eternal pain and suffering for bad people as visualized by mainstream Christianity and mainstream Islam? Or is it the reaching of a higher state of consciousness as expressed by Chopra and much of Eastern mysticism? Or is it simply returning again and again to a physical life on earth until a higher state of consciousness is obtained, as suggested by popular views of reincarnation?

As cited earlier in this book, *The Urantia Book* claims that surviving souls do not return to earth after physical death. Does this statement reveal the truth? Do these souls journey to a vast number of other worlds in the universe, continually gaining knowledge with a purpose of becoming perfect and serving God throughout eternity? Which view is true?

Or is the next life something else, even possibly a non-existent ideal? Only a living faith can determine what one's answer will be in this life.

13 ODDITIES AND POTENTIALITIES

The number thirteen has long been considered unlucky and the superstitious make an effort to avoid it. When combined with Friday, some see this as the single unluckiest day of the calendar. Where did the idea of thirteen or Friday the thirteenth to be items of caution come from? No one really knows for sure, but in 1911 it was recognized as a phobia called triskaidekaphobia.

Building owners will sometimes avoid numbering a floor thirteen – going instead from twelve to fourteen. Yet, while many people accept the idea of thirteen being a number to be wary of, others have associated it with good fortune. Such as in sports, some of the great names have worn the number. In basketball, Wilt Chamberlain wore it; in baseball, Alex Rodriguez; in football, Dan Marino.

Wikipedia's article on the number thirteen (accessed March 28, 2010) reveals the importance of this number in some religions:

Christianity – Tradition has the traitor, Judas Iscariot, as the thirteenth person to sit down for the Last Supper. Also, the supposed apparitions of the Virgin of Fatima in 1917 were said to have taken place six times on the thirteenth of the month.

Hinduism – The thirteenth day after death, a feast is held for the "peace of the departed soul."

Judaism – Thirteen is recognized as the age at which a boy takes responsibility for his actions and through a ceremony called Bar Mitzvah becomes a son of the commandments.

Becoming a daughter of the commandments is known as Bat Mitzvah. Previously, this took place for girls at age twelve; but some synagogues have changed the age for girls to thirteen. Other areas of importance for the number thirteen in Judaism: Maimonides attributed it as the number of principles of Jewish faith; the Torah says God has thirteen attributes of mercy; and kabbalistic teachings have thirteen circles, connected to each other by single lines, that make up Metatron's cube, an important geometric pictograph in some esoteric and occult sources.

So it seems the number thirteen has the potential to be thought of as either lucky or unlucky, either good or bad, and either normal or mysterious. Similar to distinguishing between cause and effect, it all depends on who is doing the thinking and the point in time when such thoughts occur: put another way, one man's oddity is another man's potential.

It appears that the unknown or supernatural offers possibilities not found in the familiar. When the human consciousness deals with the supernatural, it escapes the boundaries imposed by the familiar. Established facts that govern the familiar, present no barrier to thoughts concerning unknown mystery or the supernatural. The mind is free to create any belief about God that it finds acceptable, that is, if it can overcome the religious conditioning of its pre-existent exposure. That may prove to be rather difficult.

I look back on my own life relating to religious conditioning. Up to the time I was in my late teens, I had regular exposure to Jewish and Baptist teachings and ideas. Around age 11, I thought the role of Jesus began to magnify the big gulf between the two religions. Although the Bible was the Holy Book of Christians, Jews limited its holiness to the

Old Testament portion. Still, I did not question that the Bible was the Word of God. That would come years later.

By age 20, not having been very inspired by either my Christian or my Jewish exposure, I drifted away from attending any religious service, except on occasion as an accommodation to a friend or a rite of passage function. That pattern has continued for the past fifty years.

In spite of this, it would be a mistake to call me non-religious. Most of my adult life I have been curious about the reality of deity and the supernatural. But like most folks, my young adult and middle age years were mainly consumed in work, family responsibilities and as much play as time permitted. But religious claims and beliefs usually spark my interest, no matter what the source. Surprisingly, the two most powerful influences on my spiritual or God-related thinking came from two sources that most folks are unaware of.

The first was encountered around age 24 while serving in the military. There, I read a book called *There Is A River* by Thomas Sugrue. It is a biography of Edgar Cayce. His was a most unusual life. As a child, he had playmates that were invisible to adults. These "playmates" are not well defined by any moral, religious or scientific standard. Until age 13 he was a poor student; then he discovered that if he slept on his schoolbook, he would somehow know everything in it when awake. Soon, he arose to the top of his class. Shortly before this school book occurrence, Cayce had told his mother that while in the woods one day, reading his Bible, he was visited by a woman that had what looked like wings on her back. Curious, he continued looking at her. The woman asked him what he most wanted, and claimed that she would give him this desire as a gift. His reply was that he wanted to be helpful to others, especially sick children. After this exchange, the woman disappeared.

At age 15, while playing, Cayce was hit by a ball on his lower spine. Afterwards, he acted very bizarrely until put to bed by his father. Then, while he was in bed, he said that he was in shock and gave details on preparation of a poultice to be put on the back of his head. This was done and the next day he was well.

At age 23 Cayce lost his voice. His voice had been reduced to a hoarse whisper. Numerous doctors were unable to help. A showman with a hypnosis act attempted to restore Cayce's voice. He succeeded in getting him to talk normally under hypnosis; but when awake, Cayce could only whisper. After several attempts, with the same unsuccessful results, the hypnotist gave up. But later, while working with an amateur hypnotist – not the same person as the showman – Cayce put himself in a sleep state, the same way he had done when he had gone to sleep on his school books. While unconscious, the second hypnotist suggested to Cayce that he describe the problem with his speech and suggested that Cayce speak in a normal manner. Cayce, in a normal voice, proceeded to give instructions that his problem was a psychological condition that caused partial paralysis of the vocal cords muscles. The cure, he related under hypnosis, was to increase circulation in the affected area by "suggestion while he was in this unconscious condition."

The hypnotist then gave this suggestion. At once Cayce's throat turned pink and progressed to darker and darker shades of red over the next several minutes. Then, the suggestion was given for the circulation to return to normal and for Cayce to awaken. Cayce awoke to find his voice restored to normal.

Soon, Cayce began giving psychic readings for others. This, he continued to do for the rest of his life. The majority of the readings related to medical problems or health issues. Later, he gave life readings that included information on people's previous lives and how those lives affected their present life – akin to Eastern views on reincarnation and *karma*.

While in an unconscious sleep state, Edgar Cayce revealed various kinds of information regarding humanity, religious belief, philosophy of living, structure of human consciousness and other things that I found fascinating. Cayce also made predictions about various future events that later came true. Some of his more dire prophecies, such as many areas of the U.S., including New York City and part of Florida being reclaimed by the ocean, did NOT happen at the forecasted time. Many of his medical prescriptions and life analyses were followed up and proved to be beneficial or resulted in complete cures. The vast majority of his work was documented; it is still available for study from an organization founded by Cayce in Virginia Beach, VA called the Association for Research and Enlightenment.

Interestingly, when fully conscious, Cayce had no knowledge of the information he revealed in his unconscious state. The source of his data explained that "the mind is the builder." It taught that thoughts are vibrations of subtle energy: that all reality originated in the divine, that all consciousness is connected and that each human consists of body, mind and soul and is linked to the oneness of spirit. The mind is a layered structure that is capable of communicating with any other mind. Cayce himself often said, "I don't do anything that you can't do." However, Cayce's subconscious mind demonstrated the ability to contact the subconscious layer of other minds. He made medical diagnoses on people for whom he had been given only their name and the location where they would be at a specific time. The location might be hundreds or thousands of miles away.

Much of the information that Cayce produced in a trance about the mind or about consciousness, parallels that of Hinduism's and Deepak Chopra's. Curiously, Cayce was a life-long Christian, a Sunday school teacher and a Bible reader. He was as surprised as others were about the information he gave while unconscious. Anyone that researches the abundant information that is available on Cayce will probably conclude that Cayce cannot be equated with most of the so-called psychics of today, that, in my opinion, are putting on an act as a means of making money by deceiving people.

There is no documented psychic, seer, oracle, prophet, or the like, that compares to Cayce. The oddity of his unconscious mind accessing other minds or possibly a universal mind is potentially proof positive that both science and religion have much to discover in the mystery surrounding the one absolute of creation. I should clarify that as far back as the eighteenth century, there are recorded cases of so-called somnambulists that diagnosed disease, some while in a deep trance, obtaining results similar to Cayce's. But the records available on Cayce are unique in volume and data.

Consequently, it was Cayce's revelations that were the catalyst in my early adult life that gave me a new slant on the reality of religious experience. Particularly, to approach supernatural claims with a reasonable amount of open-mindedness, while evaluating such claims with available pertinent facts. For the first time, I began to question long-held views that had been taught in my previous religious exposure. For example, the Bible is the Word of God. If Bible-reading is approached with this belief as a pre-existent mindset, one will ingest biblical text differently than a normal book. That is why some people have read Genesis, for instance, many times without being aware of the conflicting order of the creation of humans and animals, nor the real reason why Adam and Eve were kicked out of the Garden of Eden. The Bible says it was to keep them from eating the fruit of the tree of life – because if they did, they would obtain immortality equal to God's and apparently God would be powerless to stop it. I'm sure that some who read this are unaware that two super-special trees existed in the Garden of Eden. One was the tree of the knowledge of good and evil that God prohibited the first couple from eating its fruit. There was also a tree of life that had no such restriction. Imagine, if Adam and Eve had eaten from the tree of life first – before eating from the tree of knowledge of good and evil. In that case, even if God did chase them out of the Garden, they would live forever, and apparently, still be alive today. Possibly, so would every other human that has ever been born.

When I came to the realization that if the Bible is approached like a normal book, and one still believes that it is God's Word to humanity, then intellectual honesty says God is either a poor communicator or an inept editor. How a few orthodox Jews could make Torah reading a full time occupation, or how some Christians as well as some Jews, could believe that reading the Bible was the best way to worship God, became a real puzzle to my mind. There was no mystery in their thought or action: that seemed to be the main way believers develop faith. From the suggestions produced by pre-established religious teachings: the puzzle, that is, was that intense Bible readers of various levels of intellect were more prone to increase support for the Bible being the Word of God than to question its conflicting or troubling sayings. I thought, reasonably, that study of the Bible would result in questions of truth. Here are two examples.

Jewish theology centers on the Exodus and the giving of the Commandments on Mount Sinai. From Exodus 20, if one reads the giving of the commandments only a few times, how could he not question a God Who – in verse 5 – punishes children for the sins of their fathers? Or the God in verse 8 that orders a sanctuary to be built for Him to live in, then goes into great detail about its construction? This ark or dwelling place of God has to be carried by physical manpower, or mule power, when the Israelites leave God's previous habitat of Mount Sinai. Recall this book's exploration of the evolution of Yahweh, from the tribal God of Mount Sinai to the one Lord God of today Who is seen as omnipotent, omniscient and omnipresent. How does one believe that as the most powerful, smartest and everywhere-present entity in existence would ever say that He would punish innocent children because of their parents' actions? Or that He needs a house built for Him to live in?

After gaining some knowledge of religious belief other than the belief of Jews or Christians, a pattern began to emerge. In all organized religion, tradition and authority produce facts that became a staple in a particular religious teaching. At some point, most followers of that religion assume the truth of said facts and will support new teachings that appear in harmony with this previously-accepted truth. After all, established truth is its own justification. What would be the point of regressing beyond its acceptance? That is, so long as new teachings or evidence can be made to conform to existing truth. However, if one's truth or faith has been set in stone, any new evidence that disputes such pre-existing truth is usually rejected or ignored.

Before I wrote this chapter I had only a vague knowledge of what the word Metatron stood for. As I researched information about the number thirteen from Wikipedia, it mentioned Metatron's cube, as reported earlier in this chapter. I then explored the titles *Metatron* and *Metatron's cube* from Wikipedia and discovered: Metatron is the name of an angel that appears primarily in early, esoteric kabbalistic text. There is no mention of him in the Bible. Various sources, however, attach importance to him by claiming, for instance, that it was he that God sent to prevent Abraham from sacrificing Isaac. Another source alleges that when God took Enoch to heaven, God transformed Enoch into the figure Metatron. Another source, the *Zohar*, suggests that it was the angel Metatron – not pillars of clouds by day and pillars of fire by night – that led the way for the Israelites during the famous exodus. Moreover – and this requires quite an act of faith, since there is no proof or evidence – some claim that he formed his cube from his own soul! Certain Rabbinic tradition deems him the most important of the angels whose duty is that of celestial scribe. Some sects of Christianity and of Islam accept him as being an angel. But where did the concept of Metatron originate? The Talmud, which mentions the name in passing, appears to make the earliest report of the name.

But where did the Talmud get its information? From rabbinic teachings and commentary.

There are actually two Talmudim: the older one was compiled in Jerusalem *circa* 400 C.E. and the later Talmud, originating in Babylon, became the main rabbinic reference text and the definitive text for all future legal codification. The latter post-dates the Jerusalem Talmud by some 150 years. In any case, it appears it was rabbinic thought, imagination or discussion that produced the first mention of Metatron. Other authoritative Jewish texts are the Misnah – the first legal codification – and Midrash – certain legal materials and teaching commentary – that are included in the Talmud; these claim the Old Testament as their foundation. The chief text of kabbala – the *Zohar,* a book of splendor or radiance – also claims the Old Testament as its source. The first known appearance of the *Zohar* was in the thirteenth century C.E.; some kabbalists attribute it to Rabbi Yohai of the second century C.E., although no evidence supports this claim.

Since the Bible gives no information concerning Metatron, we might wonder what is the truth about this alleged figure. Is he real? Did he exist? Is it correct to consider him as a possible example as to why certain widely-accepted religious truth or other truth should not necessarily be accepted *a priori?* Reality indicates that 1500 years ago or so a rabbi or other Jewish leader imagined a figure labeled Metatron and this figure became established by virtue of subsequent claims – unsupported by evidence – of his importance to certain people. Of course, a rabbinic apologist could easily neutralize any challenge to Metatron's existence; all the apologist need do is claim that the rabbinic figure that first mentioned the name was inspired by God to do so. Then, in the latter scenario, the figure may take on the same validation as the Bible. Said another way, each view is its own justification because each view "comes from God."

So, be it a simple number such as thirteen, a supernatural angel called Metatron or a complex human being like Edgar

Cayce, once unexplained oddity sets them apart from their kind, the potential for mystery abounds. Thus, the enigma of Edgar Cayce was the first powerful influence on my spiritual exploration.

There was a second major influence. It was *The Urantia Book*. Considering the amount of information already utilized in this book from that source, that probably comes as no surprise to the reader. The reason I've been able to quote so much from this source without documented permission is because, as stated previously, it has no copyright protection for the English version: this attribute places the English version in the public domain. Anyone can quote freely from it by merely acknowledging the source.

But before continuing with more commentary on *The Urantia Book, consider* some oddities that are most important elements in Judaism today. Yet they are not mentioned in the Old Testament: that is, the presence of rabbis and synagogues. Instead, the Old Testament has priests, rituals and sacrifice as the necessities for worshiping God. Today, it's rabbis, rituals, prayers and synagogues. Why the change?

For almost 1,000 years, Jews worshiped as the Bible outlined, with sacrificial offerings of animals in the Temple at Jerusalem. The first Temple lasted nearly 400 years before being destroyed. Seventy years later, the second Temple was completed; it stood for roughly 600 years before being destroyed during the Jewish war with Rome in 70 C.E.

This great tragedy led in Jewish history to the wide disbursement of many Jews. The Romans again conquered the Hebraic people in 135 C.E., thus ending all hope of rebuilding the Temple in Jerusalem. Jewish scholars and scribes were the ones to take action to fill the terrible void in Jewish life as they began to redirect the process of Jewish worship. Synagogues replaced the one centralized temple. Prayer replaced sacrifice. The teacher, who stressed the importance of the Torah as the foundation of a regenerated Judaism, replaced the priest. This teacher of Torah was known as a *rabbi*, meaning master.

Thus, rabbinic Judaism became the new authority for all future direction of Jewish worship and the nearest synagogue replaced a trip to the Temple in Jerusalem in order to participate in religious ritual.

I should explain that synagogues were not the result of a missing Temple. Synagogues were known to exist in Egypt as early as the third century B.C.E. They were community centers similar to synagogues of today where the Torah was read and someone gave a lecture or sermon, and they also served as a place for social functions. It is not known precisely what role prayer played in the early synagogues. The main event of Jewish worship was sacrifice at the temple in Jerusalem. However, with no temple, which was the only acceptable place to perform sacrifices, the prayers established by wise Jewish leaders became the central object of worship, thus replacing sacrifice. Perhaps competition from a fast-growing Christianity that taught that Jesus' one-time sacrifice removed any need for future sacrifices had a strong influence on the rabbinic redirection that ended the need for sacrifice. And this is a short history of how Jewish worship of today is rather different than that given in the Old Testament.

Returning to *The Urantia Book*, it surely can be classified as an oddity: it has highly unusual information and its exotic authors offer the potential to be either epochal revelation or fraud. The book itself claims to be the fifth epochal revelation to the planet earth. It claims the other four, in chronological order, as:

The Dalmatian teachings. A planetary prince and his staff came to earth about 500,000 years ago as the earth's first cosmic ruler. He established a headquarters at a city named Dalmatia that was situated in the Persian Gulf region. This group was said to be first to teach a concept of first source and center, or God.

The Edenic teachings. Adam and Eve came to the earth less than 40,000 years ago. They originally lived in the Garden of Eden. They again taught the concept of God the Father of all people.

Melchizedek of Salem. His chief teaching precepts were faith and trust in God. He is identified previously in this book as the teacher of Abraham.

Jesus of Nazareth. He taught the concept of God, for the fourth time to the world, as the Universal Father. The essence of His teaching was love and service.

The Urantia papers are said to be the most recent presentation of truth to us. Also, it is said that they differ from all previous revelations in not being the work of a single author. I would add that at least some of the papers were said to have been given in writing. To quote from page 1008: "But no revelation short of the attainment of the Universal Father can ever be complete. All other celestial ministrations are no more than partial, transient and practically adapted to local conditions in time and space."

The Urantia Book makes it clear that human religion has a natural origin from evolutionary experience. It says on page 1003: "the evolution of religion has been traced from early fear and ghosts down through many successive stages of development, including those efforts first to coerce and then to cajole the spirits. Tribal fetishes grew into totems and tribal gods; magic formulas became modern prayers. Circumcision, at first a sacrifice, became a hygienic procedure."

Thus, we are told that human experience produced religion over the course of time, but that more complete truth has been revealed to humankind in five epochal revelations. Of particular note is the concept that all celestial revelations are practically adapted to time and conditions. So, until one completes the long journey to attaining God, one's truth can be no more than partial.

The question, then, is *The Urantia Book* a true celestial revelation or is it a fraud? This was partially answered earlier by a comparison to the Bible. It all comes down to individual faith. Surely the Bible is a mix of truth, fact and fiction. My own feeling – faith would be too strong a word – is that *The Urantia Book* fits that same mix. The book, for instance, makes the claim that the divine Being that incarnated on earth as Jesus of Nazareth originally began the organization of our local universe that now contains our earth and millions of other planets some 400 billion years ago. By any standard in today's reality, that is a fantastic statement. Modern science says the age of the oldest observable thing in the universe is less than 14 billion years old. But if an intelligent consciousness was responsible for the universe's creation, that age would not address the time when preparation for its creation began. Also, scientific instruments cannot see beyond a certain point, due more or less to the natural curvature of space. At some future time, science may develop new instruments and methods that possibly reveal a much greater age to the universe. Ponder this: if the theory of the multi-verse is correct in that there could be an endless number of other universes that our scientists can never observe, then there could possibly be universes that have an age of trillions of years.

My main point is that, fantastic as any claims about supernatural beings, their activities or their ages may be, we cannot rule out the possibility of truth. Just like no one can rule out the possibility that God exists. What we *can* do is speculate or guess.

My speculation is that *The Urantia Book's* initial information was provided through the unconscious Edgar Cayce from the source Cayce was able to access in his deep sleep state. If Cayce was not the sleeping subject, then another person while unconscious was able to contact a similar or even the same source. As a practical matter, human thinking would consider such a source supernatural, diabolical or at the very least non-human. So, to describe information from this source as 'celestial revelation,' seems at least on the surface to be a possibility and until it can be proven otherwise, it is not unreasonable to accept the information as truth.

What is more problematic, to my thinking, is not unknown and presently unknowable evidence of supernatural beings, worlds, events or humanity's relation to deity; rather, it is that any seeming fantastic claim is attached to an otherwise normal human being.

The Bible's story of Methuselah's and his relatives' long lives was previously questioned. There is a man in *The Urantia Book* that has a lifespan attributed to him that vastly exceeds Methuselah's 969 years. His name is Amadon. How long did he live? According to the book, he lived over 450,000 years on earth before he was "translated" to another world. He may still be alive, as the book gives no further details on Amadon's next world experience. How could anyone believe a human being could live hundreds of thousands of years? The story goes that Amadon was a regular person living on earth at the time the planetary prince and his staff came to earth and set up operation in the city of Dalmatia. Dalmatia is already cited as the location of *The Urantia Book's* first epochal revelation. Among the prince's staff were one hundred special corporeal beings. They were superhumans that received a life plasm from 100 humans on earth. These same humans – that donated their germ plasm to the superhumans – had "introduced into their mortal bodies the complement of the system circuits, and thus were they enabled to live on concurrently with the staff, century after century, in defiance of physical death."

Amadon was one of the humans that received this special modification and he is the one ' the book gives the most details on. While the book never specifically says that Amadon left the earth after living on it for over 450,000 years, it does say that the planetary prince named Caligastia was in charge of the earth and everything went well for 300,000 years. Then, a planetary rebellion occurred. That's another story that will not be addressed in this book. After the rebellion, *The Urantia Book* says that Amadon remained on the earth with his superhuman superior named Van – for over 150,000 years. Since Amadon was modified to defy physical death, when the prince and his staff first arrived, that accounts for at least a 450,000-year life span.

So can human thinking accept a man being modified by celestial beings to have immortal life? Or that a divine Personality began the universe's creation 400 billion years ago? Surprisingly, the action of a divine Personality hundreds of billions of years ago seems the more believable.

Most people believe that God always has been and always will be. Thus, it should not be much of a stretch to think that God created divine beings for a purpose that began even more than 400 billion years ago. However, knowing that human bodies rarely last 100 years, it seems a tremendous stretch of imagination to think that even with a celestial modification, a human body could become immortal.

Yet, many believe that the physical body will be resurrected in the hereafter and then it will last forever. Perhaps Amadon's modification was similar to the same technique as that to be used in the hereafter. I do not believe that, but the potential exists for those who do. A divine Personality that has an endless age appears more believable than a human body being modified for immortality, at least, to me.

It is understandable that the Bible may contain some fiction as it has human authors. But why should celestial revelators, especially in an epochal revelation, tell us anything that is not true? *The Urantia Book* itself, as previously stated, says that its cosmology is not inspired and future scientific discoveries require cosmological updates. It also says that "the historic facts and 'religious' truths of its presentations will stand on the records of the age to come." This chapter has already addressed another qualification: that all celestial revelations are practically adapted to select time and conditions, so present truth can be no more than partial. The problem for me with those qualifiers is in sometimes distinguishing between cosmology and religious truths. For example, when *The Urantia Book* says that Jesus began His creation of our universe 400 billion years ago: this seems to me both a cosmological statement as well as a religious statement.

Even more troubling is that *The Urantia Book* makes the point that its revelators are not allowed to disclose unearned knowledge; that justifies the fact that accepted science during the period of revelation is utilized and, in the future, new discoveries will require cosmological updates. The problem is many things are said in the book that relate to science that were not a part of scientific knowledge, either then or now, and some have been proven to be wrong. A lot of otherwise unknown things are disclosed in *The Urantia Book* that appear to have no humanly earned basis, nor do they pertain to spirituality. Some of these are about numerous mortal, super mortal and immortal beings and some of their abilities. Among many other things, we are informed that in our local universe less than three percent of the inhabited worlds are occupied by "non-breathers" – mortal, intelligent creatures and animals that survive in a world, such as our moon, without water or air. In any case, even though the book had a strong influence on me and provides a lot of useful information as concerns my religious exploration, I want to state plainly that I am skeptical about some of its reported history and some of its content.

Earlier I said that I thought much of the book's information came from a source like that of Edgar Cayce. What about the rest of its text? There is confusion about how, when and from whom the information was received. It is reported that for about twenty years it came from the sleeping subject. Then around 1925 to 1927, written papers began to appear. The first contact Dr. Sadler had with the sleeping subject appears to be in 1906. It would be almost fifty years later before the book was published.

During many years of this period, Sadler headed a group called the Forum. The group met regularly for the purpose of discussing the Urantia papers and to suggest questions to ask the revelators. Supposedly, some of the communication was directly with the revelators rather than with the sleeping subject. Over the life of the Forum, almost 500 different people participated.

Imagine a revelation involving nearly fifty years and the participation of 500 people! Although Dr. Sadler was in control and was instructed to keep the papers inviolate, there is now no question that some of the text in *The Urantia Book* is the product of human authors. In fact, it is now known that a large number of published authors were borrowed from without being credited in *The Urantia Book*. This offers the possibility that information from Casey was obtained in the same way. If *The Urantia Book* is an epochal revelation to humankind, I have to believe it also contains much human imagination. Obviously, Dr. Sadler was in the best position to do the most editing and tinkering with its content.

Martin Gardiner's *Urantia* is a 445-page book that skillfully presents a skeptical view regarding *The Urantia Book*. Gardiner had to invest much time and research in his book's composition. As I read it, I wondered why a prominent science writer would devote such effort to put forth a skeptical view of a little-known book. On page 407 Gardiner gives the answer: "I wrote this book because I found Urantianism to be almost as funny as Mormonism, Christian Science, and Sun-Moonism." His reason made me curious about Gardiner's religious views. Consulting Wikipedia, I had three surprises: the first was that he was a theist, a believer in a Creator-God that does not exclude revelation; also, it was reported that he was skeptical of organized religion. Sadly, I learned that Gardiner died May 22, 2010 at the age of 95.

I now turn to a major difference between the Edgar Cayce readings and *The Urantia Book* on the subject of the hereafter. That difference is reincarnation. The Cayce readings strongly support it. *The Urantia Book* plainly rejects it. So why did I say earlier that I believe Cayce was the sleeping personality associated with the book? I think this may reflect editing of information received from Cayce. The Cayce readings expressed reincarnation in agreement with common Eastern views, but with the addition that heavenly bodies in our solar system exert an influence preparing the soul, between lives, for its next incarnation on earth. And after one's soul has completed its education by incarnating many times on earth (working out its *karma*), it then goes on to other worlds and universes.

I think reincarnation within our solar system was simply edited out, in preparation of *The Urantia Book*, instead presenting the immediate hereafter as going on to other worlds outside our solar system. I agree with Gardiner's view that Dr. Sadler was the final authority on the book's content, also that Sadler probably thought he had been "indicted" by the revelators to make improvement changes prior to publication.

I should add that the Cayce readings and the book also disagree about the origin of the soul. The readings say all souls were created in the beginning. The book has each soul coming into being with each human life. There are, however, many areas where the Cayce readings and *The Urantia Book* agree about information that is not found in the Bible. They also agree about some non-Christian teachings, even though it is fair to say that both the readings and the book are predominately Christianized presentations. Both make references to Jesus as the Master, and also as Michael. Both sources say Jesus' youngest sister was named Ruth – if true, that would be significant, as I am not aware of this being a prior claim. In any case, anyone wanting more details on similarities should read the book *Edgar Cayce And The Urantia Book*, previously mentioned. The Cayce readings and *The Urantia Book* actually concentrate mainly on different subject matter.

As all the information given by the sleeping Edgar Cayce was in response to the questions asked, it would not be surprising that two unrelated groups – Sadler and associates, the other group being Cayce's family and friends – had different purposes that resulted in many different questions and answers, which was surely the case even if Casey was not the sleeping subject of both groups.

The next chapter will explore if the information from the Cayce readings or *The Urantia Book* should be considered holy.

14 MEANING AND VALUE

The year was circa 1800 B.C.E. The place was a city in the Middle East. A man named Lot lived with his wife and two daughters. His claim to fame lay in the fact that he was the nephew of God's chosen person of that time – a time when God was very angry with the sinful inhabitants of the city and surrounding area where Lot lived. God was so angry that He sent two angels to destroy the people of the area.

As the angels, who were disguised as men, approached the entrance to the city, they encountered Lot. He recognized the men as strangers and invited them to his home for food and lodging. After some reluctance, they accepted Lot's invitation.

After they arrived inside his home, there was a knock at the door that led to the discovery that every man, both young and old, in the entire city was standing outside Lot's house and demanding that the strangers come with them so they could engage in sexual acts. Apparently, every male in the city was bi-sexual or homosexual. Lot attempted to protect his two guests by offering his own two virgin daughters to the crowd so they could do whatever they pleased to his daughters, just so long as the strangers were left alone. But the male crowd, preferring homo-sex over hetero-sex, rejected Lot's offer and began moving toward his house in order to seize his guests. Suddenly, the disguised angels reached out and pulled Lot into the house. They also caused a bright light to blind the entire crowd.

The angels then told Lot about the coming destruction and told Lot that he and his family should go immediately to a small nearby town. There, Lot, his wife and two daughters would be spared because the destruction would not extend to that town. Additionally, the angels offered clemency to

179

Lot's future sons-in-law. However, the two sons-in-law-to-be thought Lot was kidding when he told them it was necessary for the family to get out of the city in order to avoid its destruction. Because they did not leave, and disregarded Lot's warning, they suffered the same destruction as the other inhabitants of ancient Sodom and Gomorrah. The instruction the angels gave Lot's family was to leave immediately and to not look back. By the next morning they were safely in the town that was to be spared from destruction. Regrettably, on the way, Lot's wife made the mistake of looking back and she was immediately turned into a pillar of salt.

After the fiery, horrific annihilation was over, Lot did not feel safe in the town to which he had fled. So he and his two daughters fled to the hills and took up residence in a cave. Soon, the daughters became distressed, thinking they would never find husbands or have children. So they hatched up a plan to seduce their father. It worked! They got their father drunk and at different times each daughter slept with Lot and became pregnant. The older daughter eventually bore a son who became the ancestor of the Moabites. The younger daughter also had a son; he became the ancestor of the Ammonites.

This, of course, is the Bible's drama of Abraham's nephew, Lot, and the latter's role in the narrative about Sodom and Gomorrah. Since it is a story from Genesis, it must be "holy." But just what does that mean? Webster defines the word holy with several usages: "1) recognized or declared sacred by religious use or authority; consecrated, as in holy ground; 2) dedicated or devoted to the service of God, the church or religion." A third definition is "having a spiritually pure quality: a holy love.

As this is an Old Testament story, then both Jews and Christians could unquestionably accept its holiness since their religions have declared the Old Testament is holy. Additionally, both religions devote it to the service of God. But how can one believe this narrative, like so much else in both Testaments, to have a spiritually pure quality comparable to my dictionary's example of a holy love?

In fact, what meaning or value does this twisted tale about Lot and his girls have for today's reality? Amazingly, my KJ Study Bible's footnote essentially explains Genesis 19:8, the verse where Lot offers his daughters to the sex-crazed crowd, this way: olden custom required a host to safeguard his guests under all circumstances. Assuming that really was a custom 4,000 years ago, it surely did not require a father to offer his girls to a crowd for possible rape or murder. Only a deranged father would make such a proposal. Since that crowd consisted only of men that were interested in sex with other men, why didn't Lot offer himself rather than his children?

Curiously, this same Study Bible's footnote on verse 33, where the first daughter lays with her drunken father, essentially comments that Lot is basically responsible for the drunkenness and incest, but sees his role as mainly passive. My comment is that if Lot was so drunk that he did not know that he was having sex with his own daughter, then he was too intoxicated to impregnate anyone – particularly when we consider that there were no other women in the cave and that Lot repeated his performance the next night with his other daughter. It seems that Lot's role was quite aggressive or that this is simply another Bible tale that was never meant to be taken as an actual event.

In fact, my Catholic Study Bible sees the seduction of Lot's daughters as a Jewish tale about the ancestors of some Israeli neighbors that was meant to ridicule and somewhat give folk etymologies for the names of the Moabites and the Ammonites. As to the verse about Lot offering his daughters to the crowd, this Bible had no comment.

Where am I going with all this? First, it is meant to answer the question in the closing Lines of the last chapter – should information from the Edgar Cayce readings or *The Urantia Book* be considered holy? Using the three previous definitions of the word holy, any information coming from these other sources that relate to God would surely be holy to supporters of that data, as it would be recognized and utilized for religious use which fits the first definition. The second definition is met by *The Urantia Book* in its claim to be an epochal revelation. All such revelation is seen by its believers as dedicated to the service of God, more accurately said, as God's service to believers. While the Cayce readings are not as specifically dedicated to God's service, Edgar Cayce's whole life history indicated devotion to the service of God. If Webster's third definition of a spiritually pure quality does not disqualify the Bible as holy, then similarly it should have no effect on these two other sources.

I will return to the meaning and value of Lot's story being included in a holy text. Before the two angels met Lot, they, along with the Lord, visited Abraham and revealed to him that Sodom and Gomorrah were to be destroyed. He first proposed that if fifty righteous men could be found in the cities, that the cites could be saved. God agreed. Then Abraham kept negotiating until he got God to agree that just ten righteous men would void the cities' destruction. Apparently, the ten were not found, as the angels continued on their mission and came upon Lot at the gate of Sodom.

At this point, the Bible had previously revealed that Lot was the son of Abraham's dead brother Haran; that he traveled with Abraham until they parted ways and Lot settled in the vicinity of Sodom. Nothing had been said about Lot's relation with God or if he was good or bad. Lot was not mentioned in the conversation between Abraham and God concerning the pending destruction. Then why was God so merciful to Lot and his family? Lot did offer hospitality to two total strangers, but that kindness pales in his evil acts of offering his daughters to the crowd and later getting so drunk he supposedly did not know he had intercourse with each of his daughters. So Lot surely was not saved on his own merit: he was saved merely because he was Abraham's nephew. In fact, Genesis 19:29 confirms this. It seems that the Old Testament strongly approves of nepotism – not only in this case of an uncle and nephew, but also among brothers as demonstrated in the golden calf story with Moses and Aaron. Remember, Aaron was the chief instigator in actually making that idol, yet he went unpunished while 3,000 of his tribesmen were slaughtered. In both instances the Bible had God ordering these events. Of course, the greatest example of biblical nepotism is found in the favoritism God has for Abraham. Abraham's descendants are considered to be a favored race, a "chosen people." But why did God select Abram – who was later renamed Abraham – for such a great honor? The Old Testament never tells us. The first mention of Abram is found in Genesis 11:26 which says Terah was his father. Then, with no explanation, in Genesis 12:1 God abruptly starts saying to Abram to leave his country and his kindred and go to the land he will be shown. God goes on to say He will make Abram a great nation, will bless him and make his name great, also, that God will bless or curse those who bless or curse Abram. In Abram, all the families of the earth are to be blessed.

Prior to this initial contact between Abram and God, the Old Testament makes no reference to Abram's merit nor does it ever explain why God chose him. The New Testament book of Hebrews makes a case in 11:8-11 that by faith he received God's favor. However, consider that the unknown writer of Hebrews penned this some 2,000 years after Abraham's time. Also, in Hebrews 11:11-12 it says that the too-old Abraham receives the power of procreation when he was as "good as dead." Genesis 21:5 has Abraham's age as 100 years when Isaac was born. The KJSB's note sees this as a miraculous event. Curiously, the Catholic Bible avoids any comment on this verse as well as on Hebrews 11:8-12. Perhaps the Catholic scholars had the same problem with Abram being as "good as dead" at the claimed age of 100 that I do. The author of Hebrews and the KJSB's scholars don't appear to factor in how long Abraham lived. According to Genesis 25:7, it was 175 years. That means after Isaac was born, Abraham lived another

75 years. That equates his life to being only a little past half over when Isaac was born. In comparing that to a typical lifespan of today, of, say, 78 years, Abraham's virility should have been equal to that of a 44-year-old man.

We also know from Genesis 16:16 that Abraham was 86 years old when Ishmael was born and that when Abraham was likely well past 100 he took another wife named Keturah, who is also described as his concubine. Additionally, Genesis 25:6 refers to sons by Abraham's concubines who are not named. Thus, Abraham must have been very effective at procreating for a very long time. Thus, I consider the writer of Hebrews who said that Abraham was as "good as dead" and the KJSB's footnote claiming Isaac's birth as a miraculous event are best described as pure hyperbole. In fact, many events in the biblical story of Abraham, if real history, as grossly exaggerated.

There are many problems associated with the story about the patriarch of the Abrahamic religions, not in just what the Bible actually says, but also in the teachings and commentary between religions and especially between denominations of Christianity. Comparing study notes of the Catholic and KJSB was meant to demonstrate this point. Perhaps a more effective example is found in the question why do both Judaism and Christianity see Jews as God's chosen people? The New Testament plainly agrees with this in mentioning Abraham's name about 75 times, most of which relate to either the value of being his descendant or as a compliment to his faith. In Luke 19:9 Jesus even confirms the value of having Abraham as an ancestor. A tax collector's salvation is credited to his being a son of Abraham. However, Abraham's offspring include Ishmael – Ishmael whom Muslims claim as a direct ancestor to Mohammed. God says in Genesis 21:13 that He will also make a great nation of Ishmael. Abraham and Keturah, we are told, had at least six sons while the Bible names only one son each from the mother of Ishmael and the mother of Isaac. Then there are children from Abraham's other concubines, even though the Bible never has God comment on these other children. Why would not all of Abraham's children be a chosen people? And consider that based on the biblical facts, Keturah's descendants may be the most plentiful and we have no idea what people they may represent today.

Perhaps the better meaning and value of the story of Abraham is not found in a "chosen people" belief, rather, in the demonstration of the folly found in fixed creeds and beliefs. Many Jews today have adjusted the old view of God's chosen people being entitled to special favoritism and replaced it with the message that God chose the Jews to be a light unto all nations by loving God and following His commandments. This may be seen as the fulfillment of God's promise to bless the world through Abraham. Surely the last 2,300 years of actual history has shown that the Jewish people have endured hardships unsurpassed by most races. If Jews were "chosen," it apparently was not for favors, rather for extra burdens.

The biblical story of Abraham is hard to follow since it is not always in chronological order. Excepting Isaac and Ishmael, the age of Abraham is unknown when his many offspring were born. But when Isaac is born, Isaac's mother Sarah wants Ishmael and his mother Hagar sent away in order that Isaac can inherit all of Abraham's wealth. If there were other sons at this time, Sarah would have demanded they also be sent away. Thus, Abraham's numerous other sons must have been conceived after Abraham reached the age of 100. In fact, intellectual honesty and reasonableness indicates the ages attributed to Abraham, his wife Sarah and his father Terah are not based on today's calendar.

For example, Terah reached age 205. Regardless what calendar was used to calculate that age, Abraham would not have reached middle age – compared to his father – when Isaac was born. Sarah is said to have died at age 127, which would have been somewhat young based on a potential lifespan of 205 years. Even giving birth to Isaac at age 91, as indicated by the Bible, would be the equivalent, today, of a woman giving birth no later than her forties: consider also that Genesis' chapters 12 and 20 have Abram and Sarai (later named Sarah) going West or to Egypt; although the two chapters have different details, the plot is the same. Abraham is afraid the ruler will kill him to get Sarah due to her beauty; so they say Sarah is Abraham's sister, not his wife. According to the Bible, she actually was his half-sister. Abraham's suspicion of the ruler is confirmed when he takes Sarah into his harem, but never has any sexual relations with her because God intervenes. And here the story in chapter 20 gets rather wacky.

But first, I'll point out that Sarah's age at this time is over 65. This surely indicates an age by today's standards of no more than half of that. A king could have his choice of numerous young ladies. It is highly unlikely that he would go after one over age 35 unless it was for political reasons to enhance his kingdom. Anyway, the Bible says it was because of her beauty. OK. The point is made that the Abrahamic ages are not valid for today's reality and if they are, then a couple having a child before reaching middle age is normal and not miraculous.

Returning to the part where King Abimaleh has taken Sarah, God came to him in a dream and tells the king he is about to die because he has taken a married woman. The king pleads his case to God that both Abraham and Sarah have told him they were brother and sister. Thus, he took her innocently, not knowing that she was married. God confirms that He knew the king was innocent, and that is the reason He did not let the king touch Sarah. So God tells him to return her to Abraham, for Abraham is a prophet who will pray to God and God healed the king, the king's wife and female slaves so they could bear children. It seems the Lord had closed all their wombs because of Sarah.

So what is wacky? First, God punishes an innocent man and all the females in his household, then required him to go to the culprit whose deception caused his trouble and get him to pray for the king's household. Second, as God spoke to the king in a dream, I have to wonder how the king talked back. Did he plead his case while sound asleep?

Consider that most present-day scholars reject Moses as the author of Genesis as well as the other four books of the Torah. Many accepted the documentary hypothesis that says that the Torah is a composition of several sources and over time has settled on the position that four main sources were combined into what we read today as the first five books of the Old Testament. Wikipedia lists the sources, dates and place written as:

The Jahwist source (J) written in c. 950 B.C.E. in the southern kingdom of Judah;

The Elohist source (E) written in c. 850 B.C.E. in the northern kingdom of Israel;

The Deuteronomist source (D) written in 600 B.C.E. in Jerusalem.

The priestly source (P) written by Aaronic priests in exile in Babylon;

The Torah redactors, first JE, then JED, and finally JEDP, producing the final form of the Torah in *circa* 450 B.C.E.

However, within the last 30 or so years, support for the documentary hypothesis has lessened. It no longer is the major model. Yet most scholars still recognize that many writers over hundreds of years were the composers of texts that were combined and the redactors (editors) produced what we know today as the first five books of the Old Testament, Pentateuch or Torah.

Thus, we don't know who those writers are, how they got their information or which stories record actual events. In view of this, a telling question is: how did any of them know what God said to Abraham, Adam, Noah or anyone else? The assumption is made that all were historical personages. Logic says, unless God spoke to the author himself, or found a way to communicate the information to him, that the writer was totally dependent on what other people told him or he resorted to his own imagination.

Consider the single most popular event about Abraham – the command from God to sacrifice his son. God wants it done at a specific place, which requires a three-day journey. When they reach the designated place, Abraham builds an altar, lays out the wood, binds his son and lays him on the altar. Just as Abraham is about to bring down the knife to kill his son, an angel calls from heaven telling Abraham not to do anything to the boy. Then Abraham took a ram that was caught in the bushes and he sacrificed it instead of his son. This story is generally seen by the three Abrahamic religions as the great test of Abraham's faith. In fact, Genesis 22:15-18 has the angel, speaking for the Lord, calling a second time from heaven to reconfirm God's previous promise that Abraham will be blessed and that his offspring will be "as numerous as the stars of heaven and as the sand that is on the seashore." Additionally, that through his offspring shall all the nations of the earth be blessed. The reason given for all this is because Abraham obeyed God, notwithstanding that the Bible has the Lord promising it all before.

The considerable repetition in the retelling of the same essential thing in the Old Testament is strong evidence that several sources were combined to tell one story as suggested by scholars.

Enough of the biblical story of Abraham has been reviewed to explore the meaning and value of the holy text that tells about the patriarch of the three religions that, combined, inform the majority of the world's religious adherents.

What useful meaning or value does this narrative really convey to have such importance to the majority of the world's religious teachings?

Returning to Lot, there is nothing in the Old Testament that ever says anything about Lot's relationship with God. And based on his action with his daughters, he certainly is not a model for behavior. His only importance is found in relation to Abraham and that he is the ancestor (through incest) of the Moabites and the Ammonites. The ancestor part is interpreted by the *Catholic Study Bible* as a Jewish tale. The definition of "tale" could mean a real story or a fictitious one. The full explanation in the Catholic Bible's footnote indicates a meaning to me that is fictitious. If so, then why is Lot even mentioned in a holy book?

Yet, even the Lord seems to have high regard for Lot. In Deuteronomy 2:9 and 2:19 God tells Moses that the Israelites cannot have certain land that is occupied by the Moabites and the Ammonites because He had given it to Lot's children. Luke 17:28-29 has Jesus speaking of Lot's leaving Sodom ahead of the fire and brimstone as an apparent example of God's mercy while inflicting His wrath on evil people.

Also, in the New Testament, 2 Peter 2:7-8 calls Lot just and righteous. Curiously, even the KJSB questions how Lot can be called righteous in view of his having offered his daughters to the crowd. This source falls back on its note of Genesis 19:8 – previously mentioned – about the code of honor practiced in Lot's time. In 1 Peter 2:5 Noah is given as an example of righteousness.

The Catholic Bible Personal Study Edition has no comment on Deuteronomy 2:9 or 2:19, nor Luke 17:28-29. It does have a note for 2 Peter 2:5-10, which acknowledges that God saved both Noah and Lot because of their righteousness. The Old Testament does say that Noah was a righteous man and that he walked with God (Genesis 6:9). Not so for Lot.

One thing Noah and Lot do have in common is that they both got very drunk, which caused evil consequences for some of their children.

It appears that Peter may not have gotten his information from the same Old Testament Holy Scriptures that are accepted today, based on the example of Lot as a just and righteous man. But if that is true, it would bring many New Testament interpretations of Old Testament passages into question.

Yet we must consider that modern-day Catholic Bible's scholars composed a study note that reaffirms Lot's righteousness. This eliminates the need to discuss the fact that many scholars dispute that 2 Peter was written by the apostle Peter whom Catholic tradition sees as the first Pope.

I suppose Catholic tradition may be invoked to justify Lot's righteousness. However, I am not sure how Lot's evil acts can be ignored, nor the fact that the Old Testament never says anything about his righteousness.

One has only to google "2 Peter" on the internet and read some of the comment about Lot, to partially understand the mindset of preachers and lay people that view Lot's value through the premise that the Bible is the Word of God. I'll give two examples of my impression of some of their thoughts. The Bible plainly says Lot was righteous and just, so I believe God – no matter that 2 Peter was written some 2,000 years after Lot's supposed time or that the Old Testament never confirms Lot's righteousness.

Taking a cue from 2 Peter 2:7-8, some explain that Lot was all stressed out from living around all those homosexual sinners. So, when the crowd came to seize his guests, in his obligation to protect them, he may have mishandled the situation by offering his daughters. Also, with the additional stress and trauma of the destruction taking place around him, particularly his wife being turned into a pillar of salt, this made Lot very susceptible to drinking the wine offered him by his girls. The righteous Lot was simply a victim of his daughters' wickedness because he was unaware of his actions. Curiously, this kind of one-sided thinking ignores the fact that the daughters experienced the same stress and trauma as Lot. In addition, they may have lost the chance ever to marry. Yet, in a typical fundamentalist mindset of making the evidence fit a belief, Lot is seen as good and the daughters as bad.

Since Catholicism today is said to be more liberal in biblical interpretation than fundamentalists, why would its scholars compose a study note unqualifiedly proclaiming an Old Testament personage as just and righteous without any evidence? The mindset of Catholic scholars is conditioned by beliefs that include the very one that drove me away from Catholic studies relating to my first marriage: that of the Church's teachings not being subject to dispute.

Turning to *The Catholic Catechism* by John A. Hardon, S.J., ponder some of those teachings:

"The Scriptures are not self-explanatory." The teaching authority of the Church is needed for explanation (page 23).

"Everything must be believed that is contained in the written Word of God or in tradition, and that is proposed by the Church as a divinely-revealed object of belief" (page 36).

The Church is divinely appointed to "determine in precise and even technical language what God has revealed and what His revelation means" (page 43).

My point being, that if I was Catholic, I would be out of line to even question an interpretation of the Catholic Church. Of course, Catholicism is not alone in the religious arena in its attempt to exercise control over the thinking of its members.

Going back to Abraham, I have problems with his story other than those already addressed. Among them are:

How he got some of his wealth. Chapters 12 and 20 related stories of the Pharaoh and this king. And in turn, God punishes them until they return Sarah. The Pharaoh had given sheep, oxen, donkeys, camels and slaves to Abraham for Sarah, yet Abraham keeps all those gifts when he leaves Egypt. In the case of King Abimelech, he gave similar gifts plus 1,000 pieces of silver to Abraham when Sarah is returned. In other words, Abraham got rich through deception and God helped him. (In reality, this was probably one story told by two authors who used different rulers. The story is also told a third time with Isaac replacing Abraham as the main personage.)

Abraham's great test of faith. When he was told about the coming destruction of all those sinners in Sodom and Gomorrah, he did his best to get God to change His mind. Yet, when God tells him to sacrifice his son, he makes no effort to save him. Instead, he simply got up in the morning and went on a long journey prepared to do as God said. There is another very curious problem concerning his "test." The Old Testament never says why God chose Abraham. Some Bible teachers point to God ascribing righteousness to Abraham in Genesis 15:6, mainly, they point to Abraham's faith. However, God chose him and had a few conversations with him before righteousness was mentioned and the great test of faith occurred about 35 years after he was chosen. The Bible has his age as 75 when chosen, as 100 when Isaac was born and I will assume the boy was about 10 when the supposed test of faith occurred. So if his faith had anything to do with his selection, why did God wait so long to test that faith?

Skeptics of religion point out that severe psychological damage likely would have been done to a boy that experienced almost being sacrificed by his father. That apparently played no part in God's decision on how to test Abraham.

So what does this exploration of the key elements in the biblical story of Abraham really tell us about meaning and value: a dictionary definition of the word, meaning: "what is intended to be or actually expressed or indicated." Value is explained as "relative worth or importance." It is obvious from the previous commentary that I and each of the study Bibles may arrive at separate meanings about placing a value on different parts of the story. The reason for this is understood in the constraints placed on the interpreters. The KJSB scholars view scripture with a mindset that it is God's Word and that everything He says contains important meaning; the Catholic scholars have more latitude, including the acceptance of the documentary hypothesis as well as pre-Mosaic sources. Although because of the logical conflicts with statements of Jesus and the apostles, Hardon's book on page 44 says that the Catholic Church's official position is that the first five books of the Bible are somehow of Mosaic authorship. That seems to be a very strange explanation from a Church that God appointed to reveal in precise and technical language what God said and what He means. Also, in Catholic scholarship God's Word is supplanted by an equally important Church tradition that is the final authority of the meaning of God's Word. Consequently, the experts twist what is actually expressed to a value that confirms their belief.

My mindset does not operate within the boundaries imposed on those other sources. I can make my interpretations of Scripture through common sense, reason and the reality of the present day and age. Thus, aside from being an entertaining myth, the story of Abraham presents a different value to me. In fact, most of my commentary arrives at a negative value. However, I do find a meaning that has real value for yesteryear, today and tomorrow. The message is that people should set aside their political and religious views that cause division and conflict so as to unite in a common beneficial purpose.

This meaning for me is not found in the life, rather in the death of Abraham. Seventy-five years prior to his death, because of jealousy and the resultant politics of Sarah wanting power to control Abraham's household and transmit all his estate to her son Isaac, she pressured Abraham into casting out his first son and that son's mother. Notwithstanding it was Sarah that originally gave Hagar to Abraham in the hope she would conceive a child for Abraham and Sarah to raise. After this, the Bible never says what the relationship was between Isaac and Ishmael. We do know from Genesis 28:9 that Isaac's son Esau took Ishmael's daughter Mahalah for a wife.

In spite of the bad family politics, Isaac and Ishmael united in a common purpose to bury Abraham (Genesis 25:9). Note that their biblical ages at the time would have been 75 for the younger brother and 89 for the older. Just imagine the brothers' unity, had they continued and that their descendants had carried it forward to this day!

Consider if the New Testament authors that chose to mention the dubious Lot, had instead narrated on the value of unity as demonstrated in later life by Isaac and Ishmael: surely that meaning has greater value, for all times, than any discourse on Lot.

Of course, interpreting biblical passages through the reality of the present day, and with an open mind that is independent of any particular religious teaching of belief, very much of the content of both Testaments could be reworded to offer greater meaning and value to present and future generations.

Today's reality places considerable meaning on the source in establishing value. The source of all Scriptures originates with an author. In the case of the Bible, assume God was not the Author working through men. What do we really know about the authors of the Bible?

Wikipedia's article, "Authors of the Bible," (accessed August 23, 2010), takes the universally-acclaimed, Christian, sixty-six books of the Bible that are thought to be written by at least thirty-nine authors over a period of 1,500 years, and includes them with ten additional books accepted by the Greek Orthodox Church's canon. Then, list them in two categories: 1) by "author according to traditional thought;" and 2) by "author according to modern scholarly thought."

Of the forty-nine pre-New Testament books, scholars and tradition unqualifiedly agree on only one author as the writer on one book. That book is the Apocryphal book of Sirach by Ben Sira. They partially agree on the books of Ezekiel, Micah and Zechariah. Tradition has the author as the same name as the title of each of those three books. Scholars see the same authors as writing only a portion of the books that carry their names.

Also, tradition sees the writer of Tobit as unknown, while scholars attribute it to an unknown writer of the second century B.C.E. The book of 1 Maccabees is seen by tradition as authored by a devout Jew from the Holy Land and scholars agree on a Jewish writing around 100 B.C.E.

As to the New Testament, tradition accepts the four gospels as bearing the name of each author in their titles. Scholars view the gospels as having unknown authors. The book of Acts is credited by tradition to Luke, while scholarly thought says it is by the same unknown author that wrote the gospel of Luke. Tradition and scholars agree on Paul of Tarsus as the author of seven books or epistles – Romans, 1 Corinthians, 2 Corinthians, Galatians, Philippians, Thessalonians, Philemon; and six other books – Ephesians, Colossians, 2 Thessalonians, 1 Timothy, 2 Timothy and Titus – are credited to Paul by tradition. Scholars accept Ephesians as written by Paul or as edited dictations from Paul. Scholars think Colossians may have been coauthored by Paul and Timothy. As to the other four books that tradition credits to Paul, scholars think perhaps someone associated with Paul wrote them after his death. Tradition considers the possibility that three separate people besides Paul may be the possible author of the problematic book of Hebrews. Scholars say the author is unknown, but almost certainly not Paul.

The remaining books of the New Testament are seen by tradition to correctly name the author in their titles. Scholars believe these books' writers are unknown, except venture the possibility that Silas, who was proficient in Greek writing, may have written 1 Peter. Also, scholars say 2 Peter was certainly not authored by the apostle Peter. Finally, scholarly thought allows the possibility that John of Patmos wrote the book of Revelation. However, he is not the apostle John or John the Elder whom tradition credits as the writer.

In summary, other than some books authored by Paul, there is very little agreement between traditional thought and scholarly thought as to who wrote the Bible. Yet, so much of the world's religious teachings and the followers of those teachings depend very strongly on finding spiritual meaning and spiritual value from portions of a text which has questionable authorship of the overwhelming majority of its content.

But many believers may object to my analysis because it is made on the assumption that God was not the Bible's real author, and in turn, if He was, the identity of the humans that God used to deliver His Words, is only of secondary importance.

That, however, begs the question: where did the belief that God is the Bible's true author originate? The Old Testament has God or His angel speaking, many times directly to human beings. So unless one rejects such conversations as fiction, then the Old Testament must record some of God's actual Words. If one accepts that as a fact, it is not much of a stretch to then accept that everything else in the Old Testament was inspired by God.

Believing that God was the author responsible for the New Testament is a little more complex. The New Testament has a voice from heaven announcing its pleasure with Jesus Christ immediately after His baptism. And in the book of Revelation, angels – as well as the post-human, resurrected Jesus – have considerable dialogue with John. These two examples would more or less offer the same basis for believing that God guided the New Testament's Authorship as that given for the Old Testament. In other words, if one accepts that God or His representative actually did speak the words recorded in the New Testament, then it is easy to believe that God is the Bible's author.

Additionally, most of Christianity – Catholicism, Protestants and Orthodoxy – believe in a Trinitarian concept of God that views Him in three equal aspects as

God the Father, Jesus as God the Son and God the Holy Spirit that is the active force representing both Father and Son. Non-Trinitarian Christian believers – Jehovah Witnesses, Mormons, Unitarians, and others – don't teach that Jesus is God's equal, but recognize Him as God's highest representative that always acts in conformance with God's Will. Thus, anywhere in the New Testament that Jesus speaks, Christians accept it as the Word of God.

So at this point, Christians by faith can reasonably believe that God guided various humans to express His Will in their own words, thus producing the Bible, and if matters were left right there, that faith alone is the basis to believe in the Bible's authorship, then scientific method could not be offered in dispute in that science must operate in beliefs or theories that can be falsified. Pure faith is not falsifiable.

However, New Testament theology is not content with leaving biblical authorship to faith. It opens the door to evidential dispute when it attempts to offer proof that "all Scripture is inspired by God" and mainly does so by pointing to that very quote in 2 Timothy 3:16.

Aside from using Scripture to validate itself, there are other problems. Here are a few:

1) An earlier chapter addressed the fact that 2 Timothy was written at a time when only Old Testament writings were seen as Scripture by early Christians.

2) 2 Timothy was elected, through a long political process, along with the rest of today's New Testament, to be Scripture some 300 years after it was written.

3) This chapter already addressed 2 Timothy's questionable authorship.

4) About half of chapter 3 of 2 Timothy is devoted to warnings about the last days and the other half to Paul's experience and teachings that instruct on surviving them. In verse 8 it uses an example of two

bad men named Jannes and Jambres who are said to have opposed Moses. There is no mention of either man in the Old Testament. The KJSB's footnote acknowledges this, explaining that Jewish tradition says they were the Egyptian magicians that opposed Moses per Exodus 7:11. And the note on that verse says that Jannes is mentioned in the Dead Sea scrolls. Curiously, *The Catholic Personal Study Bible* acknowledges the two men as magicians named in Jewish, Christian and pagan writings, then concludes their origins were legendary. In other words, the book of 2 Timothy is supposed to be the Word of God, yet verse 8 has no more validity than the angel Metatron discussed previously, since each take root in Jewish tradition. And, of course, all Christianity rejects Jewish tradition in the latter's view of Jesus not being the Messiah, as well as on other issues.

5) Verse 12 effectively says all who want to live a Christian life will be persecuted (as do other New Testament verses). This was written in the context of an author who believed the last days were at hand. History, however, has proven that all Christians have not been persecuted. In fact, during a majority of the 1,900 or so years since this was written, many Christians were in a position to, and did, persecute others. If God inspired this verse, then it seems He was unable to correctly predict the future.

6) The book or epistle of 2 Timothy is presented as a second letter of Paul to Timothy. In verse 15 Timothy is essentially told that since childhood he has known the Holy Scriptures that instruct for salvation through faith in Jesus. It would take the development of Christian theology to promote the idea that the Old Testament has prophecies of Jesus. Yet, even today there is no plain passage in the Old Testament that instructs on salvation through faith in Jesus. It is

only by reinterpreting traditional Jewish explanations of their Scripture that Christian theologians twist those same Scriptures into evidence to fit Christian teachings. This is apparently what the author of 2 Timothy did when he penned verse 15.

So, when verse 16 is offered as proof that God inspired the Bible, does this exploration of chapter three support that statement? Even so, only weak theological claims can utilize verse 16 as proof of anything in the New Testament. For instance, some theologians use New Testament verses that erroneously quote other New Testament verses as Scripture, such as 1 Timothy 5:18's use of a saying from Luke 10:7 that is attached to an Old Testament verse (Deut. 25:4). This is a demonstration that Christians were already accepting writings that would become Scripture hundreds of years later.

Thus, when it comes to meaning and value, particularly as understood from accepted Holy text, different religious conditioning appears to offer a great variety of meanings. Only the individual can accept a meaning and assign a value that is useful in his own life.

Consequently, one person's holiness may be another's hooey. And the story of Abraham shows that God never tells him anything about a hereafter. In fact, the story indicates that God rewards His chosen and obedient with material possessions in this life. Perhaps earlier Scripture is what caused confusion for the author of Ecclesiastes.

15 REVIEW

The purpose of this chapter is to review the previous fourteen chapters and add commentary that may be useful. I will attempt to do that with a mindset that says a human being's absolute truth is limited to knowing that he is here and that he must die. All other human knowledge is partial. Consequently, everything else humans believe or think is actually selective knowledge. Scientific method does not require an absolute in its ongoing search for reality.

Most religious philosophy, however, insists on an absolute that resides outside the physical senses. The most popular description of religious absolute is called God, while some philosophies go a step further: for instance, Hinduism in its concept of Brahman and kabbala's concept of the *ein sof*. The latter two absolutes of creation are said to have imagined or created God.

Nonetheless, my mindset says that all human claims of philosophy, religion and science are, in reality, partial and thus selective knowledge.

Chapter one explores conflicts with truth that focus mainly on biblical teachings and meanings that in my mind are seriously flawed. Both Old and New Testament teachings are questioned, due mainly to conflict between biblical verses. The end of the chapter stresses the importance of Jesus' two greatest commandments that had long existed as major teachings in the Jewish religion. At this point, since the New Testament has Jesus Himself declaring in plain language the two greatest commandments, I have to wonder why Christian theologians chose to relegate Jesus' commandments to secondary importance, then, in turn, focus primarily on the teachings of Paul and his associates. In that Jesus' death was the atoning sacrifice for sin and that that must be believed in order to obtain salvation, particularly since at best the four gospels have Jesus making only vague references to such an instruction.

As a supplement to chapter one on the Old Testament, I wonder why that – possibly – its two most important characters, Abraham and Moses, show no knowledge of a hereafter. And the prophets that came after them only make a few ambiguous statements on the possibility of an afterlife, of which none made mention of a specific heavenly hereafter.

Perhaps the very beginnings of chapter one that describes the emotional minds of fourteen-year-olds say something about religious belief. In 1951 the terms 'flying saucer' or 'flying disc' and their association with alien creatures, had come into popular use within the past few years, due primarily to two events in 1947. The highly publicized happening near Roswell, New Mexico, of the crash of a reported unknown craft that was initially said to be a flying saucer from outer space. Additionally, a few days prior, the term 'flying saucer' or 'flying disc' had been used by newspapers in reports about Kenneth Arnold and his encounter with unidentified flying objects he saw in the sky while piloting his plane. After that, the terms 'flying saucer' and 'flying disc' became interchangeable. And after Roswell, both terms became strongly associated as space craft controlled by alien beings.

Four years later my friend and I saw the movie about an alien creature that crashed on the earth. By then, much of the population had come to believe that beings from space could have been visiting us. The reality of the problems that accompanied such a belief were not considered by most believers, mainly because of insufficient knowledge. The majority mindset of the time knew that any long distance travel required a vehicle. In the case of space travel, that meant an aircraft. Common sense dictated that familiar aircraft could not navigate space between planets. But flying saucer-shaped crafts were totally unfamiliar. The latter's mysterious potential allowed for technology that could be hundreds of years ahead of earthly knowledge.

During the last 60 years, anyone that became knowledgeable of related scientific facts was most likely to believe that only earth contained intelligent life within our solar system and that our having visitors from outside our solar system was a much more remote possibility. Today, I suspect that the majority of fairly-informed people doubt the idea that earth has had alien visitors. Consequently, most doubters would now require substantial evidence to change their mind.

A link may be seen between religion and ufology. In 1952 the acronym UFO – from unidentified flying object – began to replace the terms 'flying saucer' and 'flying disc.' The crash of an unknown flying object near Roswell, New Mexico was reported to be a flying saucer. At the time, those objects had very recently entered the public consciousness as things of great mystery. Within days of the crash, the military officer that was in charge of the investigation said that his initial report was a mistake. What really crashed was a high altitude weather balloon. However, much of the population was not about to give up this great mystery based on a simple fact. Perhaps even more interest was created by people believing that the military was attempting to cover up a great historical event.

Thus, over 60 years later, there are supporters for three main positions: first, that an alien craft did crash and that the military recovered technology that through reverse-engineering produced a giant leap in knowledge that allowed us to go to the moon and to make rapid advances in electronics, especially computer technology. Second, others believe that what fell to earth was a weather balloon or equipment that was not meant to be made known to the public. Lastly, some believe that whatever crashed, the military has used the event as a tool of dis-information to cover future tests of experimental aircraft. In any case, no hard evidence has entered the public domain to conclusively support one belief over the others.

In the times of early humans, so much was unknown. As time evolved, humans learned to explain former mysteries more and more. But to this day, the mystery of the origin of life as well as the First Cause of all creation, remains unsolved. Thus, presently there are supporters for three main positions: 1) God is the Originator; 2) nature is responsible; and 3) others believe neither of these and remain agnostic. The majority accept the God solution and over time have created holy texts and explanations to inform us about the originator and most reveal what He expects from us. Be it the UFO event or the origin of life, the answer of real value pertains to the question: which position is true? In the UFO crash there is surely evidence to determine that. It is, however, only available to a very limited number of people. Yet the origin of life remains, perhaps, our greatest mystery. In either case, so long as mystery exists, explanations will cover the gamut of holiness and hooey. However, validation of a hereafter for human consciousness is only possible *if* there is a next life.

Moving to chapter two, that continued to explore the relationship of biblical verses and reality, I would add to the information given on Paul and Luke by suggesting that the book of Acts was likely written many years after Paul's death. To me, this also suggests that Acts' author noted the absence of any special conversion details in Paul's writings and, therefore, created the dramatic conversion event of Paul on the Damascus road, then used Paul to describe the experience three times in Acts.

Additionally, I will further comment that the Old Testament atrocities that were justified as commands of God really seem wacky if the same mindset accepts that same God as the smartest, most powerful, most knowledgeable, and most available entity in the universe. It appears even crazier when God's great attributes of love and mercy are included. I will also note that a God with these described characteristics seems totally out of harmony with Christianity's teaching of salvation: that of the only perfect being on earth, Who is really

God's only Son, being required by His Father – the greatest Being in all existence – to endure an agonizing death on earth. And to what end? So the Father, after thousands of years, can finally forgive sin that came into the world from God's very first human creation. So much religious teaching does not harmonize God's believed qualities with His claimed will and action.

Chapter three explored religious teachings of two denominations that are not in harmony with mainstream Christian beliefs. Mormonism's founding prophet, Joseph Smith, offers possibilities that are not to be had with the biblical prophets, that is, the availability of secular history to measure the credibility of Smith and his teachings. I already said that there is much information available that questions Smith's credibility, also that a particularly revealing source is David Persuitte's *Joseph Smith and the Origins of the Book of Mormon*. Persuitte offers ample evidence to show that much of the Book of Mormon was not translated by Smith from golden plates given him by an angel, as claimed; rather, Smith was inspired by a book authored by a Vermont pastor named Ethan Smith. The latter's book was *View of the Hebrews: or the Tribes of Israel in America*. Page 30 of Persuitte's book tells of variations in the accounts of Smith's vision in which the angel gave him information on the golden plates. In one version, the angel's name is "Nephi;" in another, it is "Moroni." Both are names of characters found in the Book of Mormon.

Persuitte's book is at odds with much of what the Mormon church has taught about its founding prophet and his *Book of Mormon*. The larger question is: if there was secular history available on the biblical prophets and other holy biblical persons, would it be at odds with much of what is taught about them today?

Factual history has also forced certain former Jehovah Witnesses' teaching to be revised, as previously discussed in chapter three. But what is more interesting to me is how the witnesses can get so stuck on Bible verses in the Old Testament about eating blood, and one verse in the New Testament that advises to abstain from blood, then interpret them to mean that blood transfusions – which became useful medical procedures thousands of years later – are to be avoided even under the potential of death for one's self or a loved child. I will note that in recent times certain non-blood transfusions have been developed that in some cases can be substituted. These are acceptable to the Witnesses' authority, the Watchtower. I suppose the Witnesses believe their stand against blood transfusions to be a strong demonstration of one's faith.

However, to me it demonstrates foolishness misunderstood as faith. The Witnesses appear to ignore other biblical verses that plainly give instructions that, if followed, would likely land them in jail or even the electric chair. For example, Deut. 21:18-21 says that a stubborn and rebellious son who will not obey his parents, after attempts to discipline him, should be brought to the town elders so all the town's men can stone him to death. Deut. 13, although variously worded by different Bibles, is a plain example of an obsolete Bible teaching that, thankfully, Jehovah Witnesses as well as all sane Jews and Christians seem to ignore. That is the instruction to kill anyone that tries to turn you away from God, or toward an understanding of a different god. This is also the clearest biblical instruction that any of the Abrahamic religions might use to justify *jihad* or holy war on different religious believers or non-believers.

Chapter four touched on the fact that holy war, in olden times, was not limited to Islam: that both Jews and Christians have attacked populations that had a different religious belief. The olden Christian crusaders had a similarity to "radical" elements of Islam today in that both have slaughtered many who professed to be of the same religion as their killers. Christians attacked other Christians; Muslims attacked other Muslims, all done under the banner of God. But Christianity, like Judaism, of today, has generally relegated holy war to the past. And according to Professor Lewis, *jihad* was originally intended to be perpetrated by Muslims only as a defensive measure.

However, similar to most religious foundations, the original teachings of Mohammed may be interpreted differently today than what he intended. All major religions have different branches that vary in teachings, Islam included.

Islam has two major denominations: Sunni and Shia. Sunni is by far the largest, estimated at 75% of the entire Muslim world, while Shias are estimated to be no more than 15%. Other Islamic groups total about 10%. On Mohammed's death in 632 C.E. a dispute arose over his successor as a caliph of the Islamic community. The resultant schism produced these two major denominations that have differences in religious practice, traditions and beliefs. Both accept the five pillars of Islam as essential rules and practices. Additionally, both see the Koran as God's holy book and comparable to Judaism's dependence on its central text, the Talmud, for rabbinic teachings on Jewish ethics, law, philosophy and history; both Sunni and Shia look to Hadith narrations concerning the words and deeds of Mohammad – for instruction on Islamic law and history – although Sunni and Shia have different sets of Hadith collections. A small number of other Muslim groups reject the authority of Hadith and look only to Mohammed and the Koran as the final authority on holiness. The main point is that all Muslims look to Mohammed and the Koran as the true sources on holiness. Yet belief, interpretations and related action vary with individuals and groups, just like other religions.

In chapter four I said there was little conceptual difference between Christian and Muslim views about the hereafter in that both teach the final destination for humans is either heaven or hell. The after-death beliefs of Islam offer additional details. The deceased that are in their graves, awaiting judgment day, will be peaceful if their ultimate destination is heaven. Those destined to hell will suffer in the grave. After death, Islam has exceptions for warriors that die in a valid *jihad:* they go immediately to God in heaven, while "enemies of Islam" are said to go immediately to hell. There are seven heavens and seven hells. The various levels one experiences in the afterlife is determined by one's ratio of good and bad deeds in his lifetime. Heaven or hell for Muslims is generally seen as a place to spend eternity. Some elements comment that since God is often forgiving and merciful, He can remove people from hell whenever He wants. Some even go so far as to say that hell may one day be vacant. Notwithstanding that, non-Muslims that are sentenced to hell are generally said to remain there forever.

Islam does not say that only Muslims can receive the heavenly reward. In fact, the Koran (2:256) says that there should be no compulsion in religion. Additionally, Koranic scripture 2:62 clearly states that Christians, those who follow the Jewish scriptures, Sabians, and anyone who believes in God and the last day, and who does righteousness, will receive God's reward.

Note that some Islamic thought on the hereafter is similar to the Catholic view of Purgatory, except that Catholics believe the consignment to hell is permanent; Catholicism holds that with additional purification by suffering in Purgatory, God's grace allows all souls to go to heaven, eventually, when sufficient atonement is made whose nature and time of duration is known to God alone. Islamic religion holds that some may gain heaven even if they went to hell upon their death.

Chapter four also has commentary on prominent atheist Richard Dawkins whose mindset appears to view reality only in terms of science and the material world. I suspect that belief in God or related religious conditioning was never a serious consideration of Dawkins' thinking. And although science has not ruled out God as a possibility, it certainly seems that professor Dawkins has.

The voices of Buddhism and Hinduism are much different than those of the Abrahamic religions, as well as much different from the position of the atheist Dawkins.

Excepting the latter, the other five voices present a commonality: it is that of allowing for the survival of human consciousness after physical death of the body. The Abrahamic religions credit life and afterlife survival to the grace of a personal God. And it is through faith in that God and doing His Will that the adherents earn God's favor.

Christianity and Islam both teach that the disobedient will endure God's wrath by going to hell, although different sects can have different ideas about the reality of hell. Judaism does not either confirm or deny the possibility of a hellish afterlife. Interestingly, of the five above religions, Christianity alone claims to offer the only path to heavenly rewards in the hereafter. The original teachings of Buddha did not include any faith in an unseen God. In fact, his teachings *said nothing about a God*. Instead, the core of his instructions pertain to the subject, not of God, but of suffering. In the first sermon he delivered after his awakening (to the mission he was about to follow), he outlined his way to liberation and peace – not to heaven. This way is known as the four noble truths, which are:

the truth of suffering;
the truth of the cause of suffering;
the truth of the end of suffering;
and the truth that leads to the end of suffering.

Buddha gave detailed instructions related to suffering and how to overcome desire, which he taught was the cause of all suffering. His method required very dedicated human activity, typically spread over what he hypothesized as many lifetimes.

Interestingly, Buddha's view of reality might be condensed to: there is a natural karmic principal that has always existed. It maintains the illusion of individual human awareness that is driven by desire. Desire, as given earlier, is posited as causing all suffering. To overcome desire allows a person to escape suffering by escaping all attachment to anything – including the cycle of reincarnation. Simply said, Buddha saw liberation and peace as freedom from eternal existence. This situation is just the opposite goal of the majority of religious teachings – that is, to achieve an eternal life of liberation and peace.

A few hundred years after Buddha's death a reform movement arose within the Buddhist community known as the Mahayana or great vehicle. It introduced the idea of bodhisattvas, or people that were to become a kind of Buddha in the future. Due to their great compassion, once they attained nirvana they chose to remain in the world in order to help others reach the same goal. A bodhisattva is thought to obtain great power. Some of them operate in both this world and the spiritual world. Bodhisattvas are now seen by some people as the equivalent of gods, similar to the Hindu pantheon of gods. Notwithstanding that Siddharta Gautama, the "Buddha," was in fact, a human being and he was accepted and recognized by others as a human being. I am not aware of any school of Buddhism that teaches the concept that a supernatural God created and maintains the universe. Thus, even though God elements were introduced into Buddhism long after Buddha's death, those teachings appear in harmony with Buddha's teaching that fails to include an omniscient and omnipotent God. Originally, Buddha's teachings offered escape from the complexity of Hindu doctrine and practice. However, over time various Buddhist schools were influenced by Hinduism, as well as by other religions. So today, elements of Buddhism offer a complexity that Buddha himself never taught.

Hinduism's complexity is even greater today than in Buddha's time. Perhaps the main reason for this is that Hinduism tends to absorb new ideas without fully discarding older ones. Thus, the continual flexibility of Hinduism offers acceptance of dualism to an extreme. For instance, in Hinduism, a creator and maintainer God of the universe co-exists side-by-side with the concept of no God at all. Both views can be accommodated within Hindu philosophy. In reality, there is no paradox, since at its core, Indian philosophy perceives no dualism, only unity. The millions of gods and idols of Hinduism that are generally understood by the Western mind as idolatry are perceived by the enlightened Hindu as just the opposite. The human imagination's creation of images or aspects of ultimate reality must not be mistaken for the real thing – the one indescribable mystery or God.

Chapter five is about *The Urantia Book*. I shall leave any further mention of it to the final chapter of this book.

Chapter six addresses consciousness and its origination, a subject about which science can give no definitive answer. Several fields, such as cognitive science and neuroscience, have made much progress in understanding elements of consciousness and the mind, while at the same time offering very different conclusions. Many accept that neuroscience can or will explain consciousness by the functioning of the brain and its nerve cells. Others postulate that consciousness may reside in a non-physical arena that is the foundation of all being. My comment is that if we do not yet understand the origin of consciousness-mind in this life, how can we possibly do anything but guess about the possibility of survival of consciousness in a potential hereafter?

Chapter seven presented three men of science who strongly embrace spirit. Deepak Chopra, whose early religious conditioning was that of Hinduism, arrives at a different point of view about ultimate reality than the other two subjects, both of whom find spirit reality within Christianity. Francis Collins had little religious conditioning in his early life; by his twenties he had become an atheist. However, due to a strong emotion that reality contains something much grander than human beings, he was able to rationalize that scientific method cannot describe ultimate reality and found his truth in the gospel of Jesus – at least, his understanding of the gospel.

Karl Giberson also finds his spiritual reality within Christianity. His early religious conditioning was that of a devout creationist. But after gaining knowledge of science, he rejected creationism and its later disguise of intelligent design. Francis Collins also rejected both constructs.

These three men – Chopra, Collins and Giberson – are typical examples of the scientifically-trained mind in that most reject the nonsense of creationism in any form, although with all their scientific knowledge and elevated intellect, they find no reason to reject spirit reality. Notwithstanding that, Chopra has a rather different understanding of that reality than either Collins or Giberson.

Chapter eight presented a view of human creation in which God is the First Cause and evolution is the process that produced humankind from animal origins. How accurate it is, is anyone's guess. I do suspect that it is closer to reality than creation versions offered by familiar holy texts.

Chapter nine explored how God became a part of human thinking that produced organized religion that devolved into three separate religions with many different teachings about the same one Lord God of Abraham.

Chapter ten attempted to explore God from a logical perspective. Even so, pure logic must be guided by one's previous experience. And any reasoning about God's reality cannot escape the influence of pre-existent exposure to some religion's ideas or teachings. One's thinking is subject to arrive at opposing beliefs. Belief may tend to accept those pre-established teachings about God, or, on the other hand, reject all or some of those sayings. Of course, a major factor – one that perhaps trumps religious conditioning – is that of scientific knowledge. This is found in the fact that most scientists reject belief in God, at least, belief as taught by the most popular views about God.

Any acceptance of God as a Reality must ultimately rest on faith in a supernatural agent that science cannot confirm. No one has ever had a supernatural experience that science has verified.

In chapter ten I gave four unusual events of my own experience. Two were easily explained through limited investigation. The other two remain more mysterious. A scientific-minded friend brushed aside my meditation experience about Lash Larue's death. His explanation was that I had heard of it while my mind was thinking of something else, probably while the fact was being broadcast from the television or radio. It registered in my mind sublimely, then came to my awareness as I meditated on the dead. However, it did not seem to me a reasonable explanation for my dream about Roger. Thus, my friend suggested this: at some time before the dream about Roger's "good-bye," I had probably heard and forgotten that he had a serious health problem. It was just a rare coincidence that I dreamed of Roger around the time he died. I had a problem accepting this, too.

The problem is I'm sure I did not have any pre-existing knowledge relating to Lash or Roger within years of either event. So I consider these events to be possible proof that Edgar Cayce was correct in saying that the subconscious mind can communicate with other minds. Even if true, that does not necessarily support proof of the existence of the supernatural. It could mean that humans have this ability, or are beginning to develop this ability. The few people that had it, such as Cayce, may be the emerging proof. Science may one day explain it in terms that eliminate the existence of a supernatural cause. There is much documentation to support that Cayce had this ability. And it is a shame that no strong scientific effort was ever made to refute it.

However, chapter eleven presents a serious attempt by a prominent scientist to show his view that "God does not exist." He attempts to make a case for believing that everything came from nothing. The transition from nothing to something, he argues, was natural, which renders God as the originator un-natural, thus, less probable. Curiously, my mind arrived at the conclusion that it is more probable that something came from a pre-existent something else – rather than from nothing.

Chapter twelve explores personal experience and the effect of suggestion in forming belief. Perhaps the difference between the personal experience of Victor Stenger and myself is a plausible explanation of why our logic produced opposing conclusions concerning the first cause of creation. Stenger had extensive formal education in science and has spent most of his life utilizing his knowledge of science in his career. For my part, I had little formal training in science and, until my late 50's, made no real effort to explore scientific matters. Stenger's knowledge and logic may support his concept of "nothing producing something" as a natural occurrence. My much more limited scientific knowledge and logic does not support that theory. Perhaps my logic depends mainly on personal experience; my personal experience tells me that science has never verified that nothing has ever produced anything. Also, science has never verified that an ultimate power or God, as a First Cause, was required to produce anything. And since cause and effect is my normal and reasonable way of thinking, I conclude that it is more logical to believe in a first cause of something having the effect of creating something else than to believe that nothing was the originator of something.

Of course, this returns us to the problem of the origin of the first cause; and if the first cause had an origin, then it is the effect of another cause. This leads to endless regression of cause and effect. It seems the only reasonable conclusion is that the first cause of creation did not have an origin: it simply eternally existed. But even that answer conflicts with the normal human way of thinking in that things have a beginning and ultimately an ending. Since the greatest philosophers of all time never solved this problem, perhaps it is just as logical to believe that "nothing created something" as it is to require a first cause.

Once again, this is all above my job level, so I will comment on religious experience. Should not a distinction be understood between religious experience and personal religious experience? Certainly, some Christian folks see a difference. For example, many who chose a religious career, such as to be a preacher, may describe that decision as a call from God. On a few occasions I have asked what that calling was like. One of the clearest answers I ever got was "a sudden, strong feeling to go into the ministry." But the distinction concerns if God was active in such a calling, or if this emotion or feeling of being called was simply the result of that person's experience with beliefs he accepted as religious.

A religious experience is generally thought to be a subjective experience described by an individual as an encounter with divine reality or God. Some say that the experience was indescribable. Some Christians maintain that simply by belief in Jesus, a religious experience may be made manifest. Of course, Jews, Buddhists, Hindus and other non-Jesus religionists must focus on another belief to manifest religious experience. In fact, others say that belief in the divine in any form might produce a personal religious experience. Thus, it appears that religious experience may well define experience with things accepted as being religious – doctrine, ritual, prayers, buildings of worship or holy people – while personal religious experience is confined to individual belief and is always subjective to the experiencer. As no two people think exactly alike, this again supports that one person's holiness may be another's hooey. This state of events also seems to say that if God is the smartest Entity in the universe, then He was surely smart enough not to have established a one true religion that everybody on earth (forget the universe) should adhere to.

Chapter thirteen's oddities and potentialities supports a conclusion that religious or supernatural belief originated in the unfamiliar. The first human thought about God or gods began in an effort to explain the unknown. For example, why did a comrade die? What caused him to forever become still and silent? And in due time he would disappear, leaving only bones to evidence that he ever existed. A physical injury or trauma may have been observed to cause the death process, in some cases; but where did the deceased's movement and sound go to? Certainly human imagination would soon come up with an invisible spiritual land where the deceased would regain his movement and sound. The occupants of spirit land were viewed as ghosts or spirits with super powers that could inflict calamity or blessings upon humans. As the human imagination evolved, all sorts of ideas about God or gods were put forth to explain the unknown. So, down through the ages, beginning with unexplained oddity, man's ideas sought to explain major oddity by positing the supernatural, which produced things accepted as religious – or pertaining to God or gods. Religious experience, in turn, was elevated to personal religious experience in which an individual found direct communication with God. The big question, as of this day, in personal religious experience where humans believed they had communicated with the divine, have they really done so? Or did the human mind simply construct the belief from its experience with things it already accepted as religious truth?

Perhaps institutional religion makes its greatest error in fixing truth to a messenger sent by God in a bygone era, whose message is accepted as an everlasting mandate in knowing God's Will. Moses, Buddha, Jesus and Mohammed are the prime messengers of their respective religions. Of course, other prophets and teachers are recognized, but their sayings must be interpreted to agree with the sayings of God's chosen One. As time, culture and human need continue to progress, we find that organized religions make interpretations that use new evidence and new facts. Organized religions respond to the new evidence and new fact by incorporating them into an already fixed truth. They also reject any evidence or facts that question that truth. The end result is that organized religion holds back the normal human way of finding truth: to continually add to existing partial knowledge through a never-ending search for truth.

Consider that most Christians would instantly recognize a picture of Jesus and if someone believed that he had contact with Jesus today, in a vision, dream or otherwise, he would likely visualize Jesus as conforming with His picture. But would that really be what Jesus looked like? Of course not! All pictures of Jesus are the product of an artist's imagination – many hundreds of years after Jesus walked the earth. The Bible does not describe His physical appearance. An apologist might argue that Jesus could appear in any form the believer would recognize, although I would argue that the imagination of the recipient of Jesus' visit would draw on his own existing beliefs to create that experience.

On the other hand, no one can say for sure if God or His designated representative has ever had direct contact with a human being. I think we can safely say that many who claim to have had direct contact with the divine were mistaken. Personal religious experience is the only way to establish faith; consequently, that does not necessarily mean that one's faith is based on truth.

Humans may find the best use of their faith is not in theological understanding, but in the practical meaning and value that that faith established in human activity. Chapter fourteen demonstrates how theological truths are subject to pre-existent religious conditioning and how many Bible verses offer no useful value for practical application today. Much was said about Lot's credibility. The Old Testament gave no reason that Lot offered anything of value for future generations. Even if he really was the ancestor of two ancient tribes, both are now long lost to history and, therefore, present no describable value for today.

Interestingly, Lot – or Lut – has a more identifiable value for Islam. Christians use the destruction of Sodom and Gomorrah as a proof of God's condemnation of homosexuality. Islam, based on teachings in the Koran, sees Lot as a prophet that was sent to preach to the people to change their sinful ways. Although the land Lot is sent to is not explicitly named Sodom or Gomorrah, the destruction is similar to that given in the Bible. The Koran differs from the Bible in another way: it claims that Lot's wife betrayed him and that both Noah's wife and Lot's wife wind up in hell (66:10). Of the twenty five prophets that are mentioned by name in the Koran, only Moses, with 197 listings, and Abraham, with 169, are mentioned more than Noah's 43 times and Lot's 27 times. Jesus, by contrast, is named in the Koran twenty five times.

The Koran does not confirm that Lot ever had incestuous relations with his daughters. Muslims see Lot as a prophet that strongly condemned homosexuality. Thus, Lot offers a specific value to the thinking of many Muslims.

The different details between the Bible and the Koran concerning Lot may offer a little insight into how easily conflict can arise when the truth is made immutable. Both Judaism and Christianity generally believe the Bible to contain the Word of God. Islam sees the Koran as the unquestioned words of Allah. Consider these questions:

If Lot was a prophet, why does the Bible fail to say so?

Why would God wait over 1,000 years after the Bible's revelations were recognized, and well past 2,000 years after the event, to reveal that Lot was a prophet and what his mission was?

Why did an Old Testament writer include the incestuous acts of Lot that are not found in the Koran? Nor would it be acceptable for God's prophet to commit such acts, particularly one sent to preach against deviant sex acts.

Why does the Old Testament say nothing about the wives of Noah and Lot going to hell?

Why did God feel it important to reveal the fate of the wives over 2,000 years after their lifetime? Was it to show that even important prophet's wives can go to hell? But that would conflict with the New Testament's teaching that a spouse's faith makes even an unbelieving other spouse holy, also their children (1 Cor. 7:14). Most Christians avoid a literal meaning of that verse and have failed to give a satisfactory explanation.

Naturally, a Bible-minded Christian or Jew would see no need to answer any of these questions, since they spring solely from the Koran that Christianity and Judaism both rejected long ago.

In turn, Muslims would find that the Bible was missing part of their belief, which they deem important, and might even be reporting false information, such as Lot's incestuous acts. The one thing that Christians and Muslims agree on concerning Lot is that his story demonstrates God's powerful disapproval of homosexuality. But when their holy book offers different information on the same event, for instance, the demise of Lot's wife, no agreement can ever be reached; to do so would require one party to acknowledge that God was not the source of all data in their holy book, else gave one party wrong information. Thus, truth that is deemed fixed and unchangeable at any point in time, even if credited as God's Word, goes against other human knowledge gained through experience. This tells us that knowledge should not be fixed to one time, that as with things: change is continuous.

It surely seems that the smartest, most powerful Entity in existence would not fix any instruction to subjects He created, to live in a universe that is in a constant state of change, not one thing in the universe is static, so why would its Creator give any static instructions? Perhaps Jesus saw the wisdom in not giving teachings as unchangeable truth in His avoidance of leaving "any" written records of His own. Surely, If He thought man would benefit from a Bible that offered eternal instruction, He would have written such a Bible.

Referencing Wikipedia's "Biblical Narratives and the Quran," we find that the Bible and the Koran each refer to over fifty of the same or similar people or events. The differences in the stories are sometimes significant. Other than those already mentioned, here are other examples:

Man is created in God's Image, in Genesis; the Koran has Adam created from dust, then Allah told him to be, thus he came to be. Muslims see humankind as created in Adam's image – not in God's image.

God cursed serpents, women and men, in Genesis; the Koran does not confirm this. Noah's family of eight people is saved while the rest of the world perishes; this is found in Genesis. The Koran holds that Noah had a disloyal son who drowns in the flood, while non-family members that are loyal to Noah are saved in the ark along with the rest of Noah's family.

The Koran has Jesus speaking when still in the cradle and stating that He was a servant of God Who had been given the Scripture and had been appointed the Messiah. The event of Jesus speaking from the cradle is not confirmed by the Bible.

Possibly the most objectionable teaching of Islam, for Christians, is the denial of the crucifixion and death of Jesus. In the Koran, Jesus was not killed, not crucified; rather, God raised Him up unto Himself (4:157-158). This Islamic belief denies the central message of Christianity – the crucifixion and its meta-purpose of humankind's redemption.

Western secular scholars generally see these differences and similarities as evidence that the Koran's composition was influenced by pre-existing traditions, while Muslims reject this as they believe the Koran to be the perfect word of God. Hence, anything in the Bible that is not confirmed or denied by the Koran, Muslims are taught to consider the information as neutral, not to be either believed or rejected. I suppose that what offers value may be utilized; if not, then it should be ignored.

It all comes down to: Christians believe their holy book, the Bible, reveals absolute truth, while Muslims believe the same thing about the Koran. Jews accept that truth is found in the Old Testament. But many groups and individuals loyal to one of the Abrahamic religions recognize that sayings in a holy book must be interpreted to offer meaning and value for the present day and age. And it is within those interpretations that many folks walk a fine line between faith and foolishness that is interpreted as faith.

So, does it really matter what Noah, Lot, Abraham, or any holy book's personalities may have said or done thousands of years ago? I say, only if their sayings and deeds help someone today to establish values that consider others in relation to one's self.

The next and concluding chapter will explore the holy and the hereafter from a practical perspective that is devoid of any hooey.

16 PRACTICAL PIETY

From the limited exploration of the Bible and the Koran in previous chapters, it appears that all three of the Abrahamic religions accept the Old Testament as scripture, although Muslims believe some of it has been corrupted and that the Koran gives additional details as well as corrects information on some of the Old Testament's people and events.

While Christians and Jews reject the Koran, Jews also reject the New Testament. Yet Muslims accept the New Testament as scripture. But, like their view of the Old Testament, they view the New Testament as corrupted while they believe the Koran offers the truth about some of the New Testament information.

Previous chapters have explored conflicting information that is found in both Testaments of the Bible. Keep in mind that English was not the original language of the Bible.

In fact, before being translated into English, the Old Testament was translated and recorded in other languages over a period of some 2,000 years. The New Testament was translated and recorded in several languages before being rendered in English, some 500 years ago, along with the Old Testament.

While various translations surely include human error – which may account for some biblical confusion – it is in the minority. The majority of contradictory information in the Bible can most probably be attributed to the original authors and the intentional editing of their words by others. In any case, no amount of evidence would likely change the mind of most evangelical Christians or orthodox Jews who have been conditioned to believe that their accepted portion of the Bible is the word of God.

By 1940 the Koran had been translated into over 100 languages. The original version had been written in Arabic in the seventh century C.E. Certain elements of Islam insist that only a Koran in Arabic represents the true Koran. The first known scholar to translate the Koran into English was George Sale in 1734 C.E.

The translation from Arabic to English, as well as the present absence of chronological order, makes for some difficult reading – at least, for me. And, as with confusing parts of the Bible, different people may come away with different understanding. However, it does seem that the Koran does offer some contradictory information. For example, a previous chapter of this book references two Koranic verses that say that there should not be compulsion in religion and also that Jews, Christians and others who believe in God and do righteousness will receive God's reward.

However, other Koranic verses disparage unbelievers. At times, this seems to mean Jews, Christians or both, with references to the people of the book (Bible) or the children of Israel. Other Koranic passages specifically name both groups. For instance, Koranic verse 2:113 says that the Jews say that the Christians have nothing to stand upon, while the Christians say the same thing about the Jews, yet both groups study the same book.

Then consider Koranic passage 5:51 which says not to take either the Jews or the Christians for your friends since "Allah guideth not a people unjust." Interestingly, I'm not aware of a Koranic verse that makes the distinction between the Old and New Testaments of the Bible, the "people's book."

Naturally, the Muslims believe the Koran to be the prefect word of God. They also believe that Jews, Christians and others have rejected that belief. Thus, it is easy to understand how Muslims view non-Muslims as unbelievers.

But from the Jewish or Christian perspective, it is difficult to understand how the Koran's message can be true that they and others that do righteousness can receive God's reward.

Consider the impossibility of most Christians to please God due to belief in the Trinity. Recall that the Koran makes setting up partners with God an unforgiveable sin. The very word Islam means to submit, while a Muslim is one that submits (to God's will).

From my understanding of the Muslim point of view, I see no way that a non-Muslim can submit to God's will through righteousness unless he accepts the Koran as God's word and also accepts that Mohammed was God's messenger and prophet – that is, considering that believing Muslims accept their Koran as proof of corruption in teachings such as the Christian Trinity or the Jewish belief that Moses was the final messenger to receive divine revelation from God as to His laws – all 613 in total.

The central lesson appears to be that, no matter what name a religion has, once all knowledge of divine truth is reduced to a fixed set of "holy" scriptures, any adherents who claim opposing scriptures are classed as unbelievers. Thus, all immutable holy text or immutable theology becomes a more likely source of human division rather than a source of unity.

If God ever intended to give humankind a set of holy instructions that would apply to everyone for all times, it surely seems that revealing this knowledge to one person, sometimes with hundreds of years between revelations, was not the most effective way to inform all the people. For example, if God gave Moses the ten commandments written on stone tablets, why were they limited to the leader of a band of wandering nomads? Surely a spectacular, miraculous appearance of similar tablets in every nation on earth would have been tremendously more effective. And all future revelations, simultaneously delivered to each nation of the world in the same manner, would have better united the believers in one God and in belief in what He expects of us in a much more effective manner than the division in religiosity that we witness today.

For those who would argue that God was very selective to find the right person to receive and pass on His divine revelations, I would ask the question, "then why Moses?" My question makes the assumption that the biblical creation story was factual. If it were factual, would not God have been smart enough to realize that once the first couple disobeyed him that if He wanted absolute obedience, He must do more than "tell humans how to behave?" This could have been accomplished by revamping the human neurological system, but that would appear to eliminate free will. So why not give the first couple a set of stone tablets that spelled out God's mandated instructions that also included that at least one parent must pass on these instructions to each of his children? Maybe, take it a step further and require every family must have and must review its individual set of tablets, say, every seventh day. For those who would argue that Adam could not read, that would be a minor detail for God to handle – since Adam was created full grown in both body and mind. I should add that free will has long been denied by some elements of Christianity. Oddly, atheistic, neuroscientist Sam Harris agrees that humans do not have free will. He concludes this based on MRI studies. The religious conclusion credits God only with free will.

The one clear point is that the smartest entity in the universe could surely have ordered a more effective plan to insure that humans did His will than any plan offered by the Abrahamic religions.

Perhaps the best way to deal with the reality of the abundant number of conflicting religious claims that exist today is to filter one's "preferred" belief through a fine sifter of common sense. Beliefs thus processed that benefit the most people at the least hardship to others would surely produce the best religious philosophy. Thus, we could navigate the fine line that many religionists thread between holiness and hooey – faith and foolishness.

True, some folks have much more productive common sense than others, even some others of higher intellect. Intellect and experience are one's sources of judgment for everything, not just religious belief. So why not utilize one's full ability to arrive at faith?

Even though the facts of science are more reliable than the facts of religion, they do not necessarily lead the scientist to always make the best decision – particularly if common sense is relegated to the back burner. I first wrote this as I sat in Starbucks. As I took a break and awaited my latté – no fat, of course – I was plainly reminded that scientific facts, absent common sense, might prove useless.

As is my habit to read anything that is available while waiting, I picked up from the Starbucks' news rack the November 30, 2010 edition of *The New York Times*. I noticed a front-page article that said extra vitamin "D" and calcium are not necessary, based on a recent study by accepted experts. Interestingly, I had recently increased my supplementation of "D" by five-fold, based on an article by the reported world's foremost authority on vitamin D.

An hour or so later I stood waiting on the overload of caffeine in the triple *viente* lattés that I was bringing to a friend. Again, I picked up a newspaper, this time a *Wall Street Journal* – also the November 30, 2010 edition. In the top right hand corner of the front page was a caption for an inside article that read "Vitamin D prescription: tripling the daily dose." Of course, this article also referenced information from experts. So, on the same day, this nation's two leading newspapers offer conflicting advice, each obtained from experts who arrived at their conclusions through the scientific method.

My common sense told me not to depend on either report, but, instead, to look for additional support before forming a belief. For those who care to know, I presently have faith that all adults, particularly older ones, should take at least 2,000 IU of vitamin D-3 daily instead of the standard 400 IU. In addition, a supplement of vitamin K, especially the two forms of K-2, may prove beneficial; although people on strong blood thinners, like coumadin, should only take low doses of K under supervision of their doctor and people with high blood levels of calcium should check with their doctor about supplementation with vitamin D.

The point here is that even scientific facts should be evaluated with a dose of common sense. That certainly does not mean that all solid scientific fact can be validated by common sense. It means that to ignore common sense may invalidate the usefulness of a fact that is produced from scientific method. And in the aforementioned opposing vitamin studies, both allegedly arrived at their conflicting conclusions by utilizing scientific method. Common sense is necessary to conclude that at least one study is flawed and more research is needed to obtain the truest result.

In the same way, any religious interpretation – even if based on solid scriptural, theological or traditional foundation – should incorporate a healthy mindset of common sense in order to produce the best and most useful belief. I might say, the latter is "the holiest belief."

It has been my observation that the most devout religious adherents, particularly recently born-again Christians, are rather prone to discount common or normal sense. They tend to read, rely on and recommend only informational sources that support their preferred belief and thus explore only one side of the issue.

One's intellectual capacity appears not to factor in the "born again" mindset. Our friend Francis Collins mentioned earlier is a good example. Here is a famous scientist that was recently promoted to one of the most powerful scientific positions in the world. He is now the director of the National Institutes of Health.

Recall that Collins' book is subtitled *A Scientist Presents Evidence For Belief*. Also, that he accepted Jesus as Savior and the resurrection as a fact. Additionally, recall that Collins was previously an atheist. Here are some of his conversion details from page 225 of his book:

A year passed after he decided to believe in God. Then, he was being called to account by something he read from the Christian writer C. S. Lewis.

On a beautiful fall day, he was hiking in the Cascade Mountains during his first trip West of the Mississippi.

He said: "The majesty and beauty of God's creation overwhelmed my resistance."

Again, his words: "As I rounded a corner and saw a beautiful and unexpected frozen waterfall, hundreds of feet high, I knew the search was over."

The next morning he knelt and surrendered to Jesus Christ.

The final conversion evidence for Collins appears to be a beautiful and unexpected frozen waterfall. I imagine his scientific mind could naturally have explained such a pleasant sight. However, for a year he had decided to believe in some sort of God. So how much of a factor was his normal common sense in his actual religious conversion? I have to wonder about Collins' reaction had he, instead, made his trip to, say, Haiti, and was hiking there on the beautiful day that the terrible earthquake first occurred that may have killed over 300,000 of some of the most poverty-stricken people on earth. Would having witnessed such a terrible, natural and unexpected sight put him on the path back toward atheism? I strongly suspect that in this scenario Collins would not have found the end of his search in this other view of God's majesty.

It is not my intention to belittle Collins or any believer of any faith. But I do not think that Collins' description of his conversion supports "evidence for belief;" rather, it is evidence for a preference *to believe*. For a year Collins had a preference to believe; he just needed to decide what sort of God it would be. Why did he decide on Jesus Christ? What was it in the "majesty and beauty of God's creation" that was the final catalyst in his surrender to Jesus?

My guess is that the beauty of nature stirred his emotions to accept the preconditioning he had experienced from reading a lot of C. S. Lewis, as well as counseling from his neighbor who was a Christian minister.

Clearly, Collins' conversion to Christianity was accomplished with a different mindset than that applied in effectively directing the genome project. A non-believing scientist with knowledge comparable to that of Collins and who had no pre-existing preference to believe might find better evidence for belief in aspects of the genome project than in a frozen waterfall. However, he would perhaps see it as evidence of evolving natural selection without a role for God.

On page 199 of Collins' book he tells us that he is enormously satisfied with the dominant position of biologists who are also believers. It is known as theistic evolution: the combination of God the Creator and His master plan of evolution regarding all living things. Of course, also accepting God's Big Bang could account for the evolution of everything else.

On the prior page Collins says he began "to perceive some of the eternal truths of the Bible," the most important truth surely being the previously noted "Jesus as Saviour and the resurrection as a fact." But I still have to wonder if Collins believes in all or rejects some of the biblical miracles! Of note is that acceptance of evolution as God's plan of creation partially unites science and religion. In the simplest terms, God created the universe and everything in it through His plan of evolution. God put His plan into play and ultimately scientists can understand how it works through study of the material world. Thus, the believing scientist need have only one issue with the scientific non-believer: that is the question, of who or what was responsible for evolution.

There appear to be three possible answers:

A. An evolutionary process has eternally existed;
B. The process came into being from nothing;
C. God, or His equivalent, created evolution.

The non-believer accepts either A or B, while the believer has a single choice. Either way, once the scientifically-minded acknowledges the fact of evolution, the believer and the non-believer alike can utilize scientific method to understand the workings of the material world. Referencing Wikipedia's "Theistic Evolution," I learned: evolutionary creation is a term that describes a similar concept as theistic evolution. Evangelical Christians that accept evolution as God's plan prefer the former term as this group credit God with taking a more active role in evolution than for most theistic evolutionists.

Wikipedia, sourcing *The Pew Forum*, reports the following percentage of believers within different religions that say evolution best explains the origin of human life on earth:

Buddhist 81%
Hindu 80%
Jewish 77%
Catholic 58%
Mainline Protestants 51%
Muslim 45%
Evangelical Protestants 24%
Mormon 22%
Jehovah Witness 8%
Total U. S. population 48%

Our favorite atheist, Richard Dawkins, considers theistic evolution as a superfluous attempt to "smuggle God in by the back door."

It may be worth noting Wikipedia's take on deism, a God belief that has yet to be mentioned in this book. "Deism is belief in a God or first cause based on reason, rather than on faith or revelation." Simply said, most deists believe God created the universe and then let it evolve without His participation, including no miracles. Some deists say God ceased to exist after putting the universal laws into play. History's most famous deist is probably Thomas Jefferson.

This book has explored many views about the holy and various views about the hereafter. There may be remnants of truth in every religion – more in some, less in others. But it certainly appears obvious, at least to me, that no religion or sect of any religion has a lock on truth. In fact, in my evaluation, I find no compelling reason to believe that any of the major religions has a more realistic view of the holy or a more factual description of the hereafter than any of the others.

If the subject of religion could be considered from a purely neutral perspective, which may be an impossibility, some teachings of every religious denomination on this planet would be found lacking.

Intellectual honesty would show that the foundation for much theology is simply human imagination or speculation. This is demonstrated by the degree of circular reasoning found in aspects of tradition. For example, the previous exploration of the appearance of the angel Metatron in Jewish tradition; an example in Catholic tradition is a teaching such as the infallibility of the Pope on matters of faith and morals. Simply said, the Catholic Church declares the Pope to be infallible because previous Church officials said he was infallible.

Any religious mandates that stem solely from tradition without any foundation in the religion's holy text are actually only the speculative imagination of religious authorities at some point in the past.

And I believe that this book has already well demonstrated that many teachings that find a basis in holy text are subject to dispute. For instance, Catholicism finds a foundation for a chain of Popes that begins with Peter because the Bible has Jesus telling Peter – after changing his name to Peter, a name that has come to mean rock – that on this rock I will build my Church. Then, in the next verse, Peter is given the power to bind or to loosen things on earth (Mt. 16:18-19). However, in Mt. 18:18 Jesus also gives other disciples this power. Most of the rest of Christianity disagrees with a papal interpretation.

In fact, the Bible indicates that Jesus said this when He and Peter were outside. A possible meaning of Jesus' words about this rock could just as well be that anywhere, even outside on a rock, Jesus' Church would be built through His message. Surely if Jesus intended to establish an ongoing leader of His church, He would not have used such an obscure message. Else, He could not forsee the future division and conflict it could cause.

As alluded to previously, any apologist for God may use circular logic to support a preferred scripture, belief, or tradition with the claim that it was inspired by God. I think a major teaching of the Catholic Church offers a plain example.

This is found in the aforementioned claim of the Church that it was divinely appointed to speak for God. Thus, anything it teaches becomes tradition and the equal of a statement from God.

Of course, non-Catholics, notably other Christians, believe that claim to be nonsense – notwithstanding that some who reject this Catholic view also teach that their own traditional claims come from God.

The central point is that regardless of any teaching from any religion or sect that is based on an authority that originated in that teaching from past, accepted human authorities is evidence founded on circular reasoning. This presents a question about statements attributed to human beings said to be speaking for God. Are sayings in holy texts, such as from prophets in the Bible, really any more reliable than those of Church or rabbinic officials?

Intellectual honesty would demand that authority derived from holy texts is simply evidence from other human claims in the more distant past that has been recorded and accepted as being holy. The reality of evidence dependent on holy text or religious tradition is not evidence generally acceptable to our legal system, as it would be considered "hear-say." That does not mean that many religious teachings are not supported by our legal system, such as not to murder. Although the Bible also gives opposite instruction as noted in Deut. 13: To murder anyone that tries to turn one away from the God of Israel.

In my mind, this book reasonably supports that any and all claims of religion should be evaluated with the inclusion of a mindset of normal common sense.

Religion is often used as a justification to commit acts that are contrary to *normal* common sense, be it the suicide bomber of Islam or the action of a Jehovah Witness that would risk the death of an innocent child in avoidance of a needed blood transfusion based on his sect's view of Christianity. The vast majority of the world's population – both religious and non-religious – would likely interpret such action as foolishness, and, in the case of a murderous terrorist, as pure evil.

Consider the maxim, "to let your conscience be your guide." This has commonly been accepted as good advice. However, some religious faith leads to that being very bad advice. For instance, in the above-mentioned examples of the J.W.'s faith against blood transfusions and the suicide bomber's faith that he is acting for God in killing the innocent. In each case, the believer's faith or consciousness has been conditioned in the name of a religion and his mind has come to believe that he is doing God's will. In other words, his conscience is saying that he is doing righteousness, while most people see it as foolishness or evilness.

Is there such a thing as "the wee small voice" which some associate with the soul? The conscience may be simply conditioned by experience and related belief in the physical world. But at a deeper level of consciousness is there a wiser director of morality that transcends beliefs formed from experience in the material world?

Most people – with or without religious belief – generally know right from wrong. Atheists are as moral as believers. Is morality inherent to human nature? Certainly individuals and cultures disagree about many things relating to what is right or wrong, or the degree of evilness. But the majority do have a natural instinct of good and evil which possibly emanates from a source beyond the more active conscience. And if so, this source might reside outside the physical brain. Yes, that is pure speculation again on my part and I have absolutely no credentials or training in the human neurological system.

But, as previously mentioned, some that are considered experts in the field point out that no one knows how consciousness originates in the brain. Recall that neurological scientists have discovered how a memory survives in the brain. However, to my knowledge, they have no hypothesis as to how an idea is created in the brain. They can only explain how an idea is processed in the brain as it is captured by numerous formations of nerve cells, thus becoming a memory. It appears most human ideas are mixtures of other people's previous suggestions that are incorporated into one's own stored memory that produce one's present thought.

The point is that human beings rarely have an original idea. Most of our thoughts are simply a combination of other human thinking. When applied to religion, this is particularly true, notwithstanding that an endless number of twists are applied to a very few original concepts of God.

However, in that rare moment when one's mind generates an original idea, where does it come from? Do some ideas, like our previous consideration of consciousness, possibly originate outside the human brain? Is there any meaningful difference between consciousness and an idea? Certainly, all ideas are thoughts processed by one's consciousness. And it seems that most ideas are structured in consciousness from experience with the suggestions or thoughts of other people.

Plato taught that all ideas were mental forms that were innate to the soul. Carl Jung's archetypes are universal forms that exist in the human mind as well as in the external world. Unconsciously, all human thinking draws on these basic patterns to form one's interpretation of conscious experience. These basic forms are naturally modified by individual experience.

If these universal structures do exist, then it appeared inevitable that ideas about God would at some point arise in human thought, also that any original conception of God would naturally take on many modifications to conform with the varied conscious experience of different God-seekers. And that is exactly what the religions of the world demonstrate today. This tends to confirm that any or all of humanity's ideas about God are partial. If God exists, there is surely no single path that He requires in order to know His will. God truth – like all knowledge – should continually evolve and cannot be limited to any claims of absolute truth.

It seems that humankind, while tending to put known knowledge to practical use and continually update its application and efficiency, does not usually do that with the central precepts of religion. One could argue that that is because God's truth was passed to man in the distant past and while man should continually interpret and make application of that knowledge, truth from God is itself fixed and unchangeable. The problem is that such a position assumes that the core precepts have been interpreted correctly and that those truths are fixed for evermore.

Secular human knowledge generally grows and progresses by applying common sense, practicality and usefulness to education and technical ability. Now use these factors to explore some religious concepts.

Consider Hinduism's teaching that the oversoul of all creation – Brahman – is everywhere present: in rocks, plants, water, air, us and everything else in existence. A common teaching of gurus regarding devotion to man-made symbols and idols is that once the figure is created, the maker then invites God to occupy it with His presence for a limited devotional period. But since God exists everywhere, was He not already present? Due to the flexibility of Hindu philosophy, one might argue that Brahman was already in the figure or idol as the impersonal aspect of all creation. It was God, the personal deity that was invited by the idol-maker. The central message here is that once Brahman is fixed for all time as the omnipresent, impersonal aspect of all creation, common sense and usefulness will require theological and mystical instruction from esoteric authorities in order for the believer to make practical application of unchangeable precepts.

I have previously explored numerous problems in teachings related to Abrahamic-based religion. Now consider a core teaching, accepted by mainline Christianity, Judaism, Islam and partially by Mormonism, namely, that of belief in a last or chief prophet that received and revealed God's revelation. For Judaism, it was Moses; for mainline Christianity, Jesus; for Islam, Mohammed. Mormonism accepts Jesus as God's Messenger, but holds that Joseph Smith was God's latter-day chief prophet who gave new revelations.

Thus, as the world increased in population, God appears to have become removed from humankind. The Bible has God directly communing with Abraham for 100 years. God spoke often to Moses for at least 40 years. From the Christian perspective that Jesus was the same as God speaking, He only did so publicly for perhaps three years and the Bible makes little mention of Jesus' words before then.

Mohammed is said to have received God's word from the angel Gabriel. Mormonism's Smith claimed that both God and Jesus paid him a brief visit. However, his revelation was primarily from an angel – never previously heard of – who provided him with golden plates.

The revelation of *The Urantia Book* was conducted by creatures named "Midwayers," that is, beings said to be a level above humans, but below angels. The first appearance of Midwayers is said to have been on earth some half million years ago. A second group was born during the days of Adam and Eve less than 39,000 years ago. These beings are invisible to humans. Over 10,000 Midwayers are said to be still active on earth. Their relation to humans is in transmitting information from beings higher on the spiritual hierarchy. On very rare occasion, they may act directly with a human.

Now, ponder Wikipedia's estimate of *World Population* (accessed 21 March 2011) during the approximate lifetime of the below revelators:

Abraham 35 million
Moses 50 million
Jesus 200 million
Mohammed 250 million
Smith 1.1 billion
1955, publication of *The Urantia Book* 2.75 billion.

Of note, when I began writing this book, around four years ago, Wikipedia estimated the world population at 6.6 billion; now, it is 6.91 billion. The increase is nearly equal to the present population of the United States that is given as just over 311 million.

So it seems that God "hides His face" as the world got more crowded. In fact, some Jewish theologians use that very term to describe God's communion with man after Moses' time. Christians may dispute the concept of "hiding His face" with the New Testament verse that has Jesus saying that "if you have seen Him, you have seen His Father."

Even if we assume divine revelation was transmitted to all six of the listed revelators, God spent less time in proclaiming

His word directly to men as the world population increased. Instead, he delegated the job to angels. And in the case of *The Urantia Book*, an order of beings just above man made the actual contact. But from the perspective of common sense, practicality and usefulness, does this analysis have any value? It demonstrates how theological claims start with an assumption that may or may not contain truth, yet can grow into a fixed precept of a particular faith. This is the result of human authorities assumed role of speaking for God and organizing a religion. So, when is one's faith really holy?

The indication of this book is that holiness is an individual belief. No authority, no sacred text or theological concept can bestow holiness unless one believes that truth has been revealed and accepts it. And even so, one's faith is not necessarily based on the truth.

Is there a hereafter for the survival of human consciousness? This book presents the possibility. But consider those who say that all individual awareness terminates forever at death. Would it really be so bad to have absolute peace and non-suffering for all eternity, like Buddha originally taught? Is it really more satisfying to have a conditional choice that results in eternal joy in heaven, but with the more likely conclusion of eternal pain and suffering in hell, as taught by Christianity and Islam? Someone may prefer ultimately returning and becoming part of Hinduism's oversoul of creation, potentially participating as an impersonal component forever.

Maybe Jewish thought that does not attempt to offer a definite view of the next life is the most reasonable – particularly since it stresses moral behavior in this life. In any case, a human being may find his own salvation by making a choice of what is holy and what is hooey in this lifetime. That is the only period in which one can really be sure of ever being conscious.

Perhaps this book's benediction should be: may God bless our planet – provided it does not upset the natural order of the universe.

AFTERWORD

One final comment I wish to firmly express. Intelligence of the human species, whether weak or strong, does not deter the acceptance of some otherwise absurd belief, particularly certain religious belief. I think Francis Collins' dependence on C. S. Lewis' writings offers a telling example. On page 224 in *The Language of God*, Collins quotes a paragraph from Lewis' *Mere Christianity* that seemed to have been written just for Collins in regard to the latter's thought that "maybe Christ was just a great spiritual teacher." It reads:

> I am trying here to prevent anyone saying the really foolish thing that people often say about Him: "I'm ready to accept Jesus as a great moral teacher, but I don't accept His claim to be God." That is one thing we must not say. A man who was merely a man and said the sort of things Jesus said would not be a great moral teacher. He would be either a lunatic – on a level with a man who says He is a poached egg – or else He would be the devil of hell. You must make your choice. Either this man was, and is, the Son of God; or else a madman or something worse. You can shut Him up for a fool, you can spit on Him and kill Him as a demon; or you can fall at His feet and call Him Lord and God. But let us not come with any patronizing nonsense about His being a great human teacher. He has not left that open to us. He did not intend to.

Collins thought that Lewis was right: "I had to make a choice." I already explored Collins' choice in this book. So what is absurd about either Collins or Lewis?

That apparently both believed that one's choice about belief in Jesus was limited to: He was, and is, the Son of God; or else He was a madman. These two great minds did not seem to have considered that Lewis' choices are based entirely on a single theological interpretation of the New Testament, when the truth could simply be that Jesus never actually did, said or meant some of the things that have been attributed to Him.

Lewis' quote is a good example of assuming a religious truth without even allowing other reasonable possibilities. I believe this book supports the choice that Lewis' quote is pure "nonsense," since it considers only one view of a very complex issue. When all is said and done, it comes down to: does a human being need God in this life? My humble opinion is: if one's faith in God leads him to consideration and concern for the welfare of his fellow man, then the answer is YES. And on the other hand, if one's faith in God leads only to the insistence that other humans *must* follow his version of the one and only path to God, then the answer is NO. Said another way: the former faith is holy; the latter faith is hooey.

REFERENCES

THE BIBLE

The Bible: Catholic (NAB), The Catholic Bible: Personal Study Edition. New York: Oxford University Press, Inc., 1995.

The Bible: Jewish, Tanakh, The Holy Scriptures. Philadelphia: The Jewish Publication Society, 1985.

The Bible: King James Study Bible. Grand Rapids, MI: Zondervan, 2002.

The Bible: New King James Version. Nashville, TN: Thomas Nelson Publishers, 1982.

The Bible: New Revised Standard Version. New York: Oxford University Press, Inc., 1989.

The Bible: New World Translation of the Holy Scriptures. New York: Watchtower Bible and Tract Society, Inc., 1984.

OTHER HOLY SCRIPTURES

The Book of Mormon; The Doctrine and Covenants; The Pearl of Great Price. Salt Lake City: The Church of Jesus Christ of Latter-Day Saints, 1977.

Qur'an. Tr. Abdullah Yusuf Ali. New York: Tahrike Tarsile Qur'an, Inc, 2005.

OTHER REFERENCES

Bro, Harmon Hartzell. *A Seer out Of Season: The Life of Edgar Cayce.* New York: The Penguin Group, 1989.

Bunker, John M and Karen L. Pressler. *Edgar Cayce and the Urantia Book.* Ft. Wayne, IN: Craftline Printing, Inc., 1999.

Chopra, Deepak. *Life After Death*. New York: Harmony Books, 2006.

_____, *The Third Jesus*. New York: Harmony Books, 2008.

Collins, Francis. *The Language of God*. New York: Free Press, Inc. 2006.

Crystal, David, ed. *The Barnes and Noble Encyclopedia*. New York: Barnes and Noble, Inc., 1993.

Darwin, Charles. *The Origin of Species*. Franklin Center, PA: The Franklin Library, 1975.

Dawkins, Richard. *The God Delusion*. New York: Houghton Mifflin, Co., 2006.

Emerick, Yahiya. *Complete Idiot's Guilde To Understanding Islam*. New York: The Penguin Group, Inc., 2001.

Friedman, Richard Elliott. *Who Wrote the Bible?* New York: HarperCollins Publishers, Inc., 1989.

Gardner, Martin. *Urantia*. Amherst, NY: Prometheus Books, 1995.

Giberson, Karl W. *Saving Darwin*. New York: HarperCollins, Inc., 2008.

Great World Religions: Five Audio CDs and Guidebooks: Buddhism; Christianity; Hinduism; Islam; Judaism. Malcolm David Eckell, Luke Timothy Johnson, Mark W. Muesse, John L. Esposito, Isaiah M. Gafni. Chantilly, VA: The Teaching Company, Inc., 2000.

Halley, Henry H. *Halley's Bible Handbook*. Grand Rapids, MI: Zondervan Publishing House, 1965.

Hardon, John A., S.J. *The Catholic Catechism*. New York: Doubleday, 1981.

Kaiser, Walter C., Jr., Peter H. Davies, F. F. Bruce, Manfred T. Brausch. *Hard Sayings of the Bible*. Downer's Grove, IL: Intervarsity Press, 1996.

Lewis, Bernard. *The Crisis of Islam*. New York: The Modern Library, 2003.

Persuitte, David. *Joseph Smith and the Origins of the Book of Mormon*. Jefferson, NC: McFarland and Company, Inc., 2000.

Reiss, Jana and Christopher Kimball Bigelow. *Mormonism for Dummies*. Hoboken, NJ: Wiley Publishing, Inc., 2005.

Schwartz, Gary E. and William L. Simon. *The G.O.D. Experiments*. New York: Atria Books, 2006.

Stenger, Victor J. *God the Failed Hypothesis*. Amherst, NY: Prometheus Books, Inc., 2007.

Smith, Huston. *The World's Religions*. Rev. and updated ed. San Francisco: HarperCollins, 1958.

Strong, James. *The New Strong's Concise Concordance of the Bible*. Nashville, TN: Thomas Nelson Publishers, 1985.

Sugrue, Thomas. *There Is A River*. New York: Henry Holt and Company, 1945.

The Urantia Book. Chicago: Urantia Foundation, 1995.

Wikipedia, the free encyclopedia on the Internet was routinely referred to and specific articles are listed within this book.

World Christian Encyclopedia. New York: Oxford University Press. Inc., 2001.